Humorous Crosswords

Cathy Allis Millhauser

STERLING PUBLISHING CO., INC.
New York

To the memory of my father, Richard Allis,
who handed down his punning genes to me

Special thanks to Terry Hackett, who put up with many a "spoiler"
during the making of this book so that I could get her wise and witty advice.

Edited by Peter Gordon

7 9 10 8

Published by Sterling Publishing Company, Inc.
387 Park Avenue South, New York, N.Y. 10016
© 2003 by Cathy Allis Millhauser
The puzzles on pages 13, 22–23, 29, 34, 42, 52, 58, 66–67, and 75 are
© 1996, 2000, 1989, 1997, 1999, 1995, 2001, 1998, and 2002
American Crossword Puzzle Tournament
(www.crosswordtournament.com)
and are reprinted with permission.
Distributed in Canada by Sterling Publishing
% Canadian Manda Group, One Atlantic Avenue, Suite 105
Toronto, Ontario, Canada M6K 3E7
Distributed in the United Kingdom by GMC Distribution Services
Castle Place, 166 High Street, Lewes, East Sussex, England BN7 1XU
Distributed in Australia by Capricorn Link (Australia) Pty. Ltd.
P.O. Box 704, Windsor, NSW 2756 Australia

Printed in China
All rights reserved

Sterling ISBN-13: 978-0-8069-8951-8
ISBN-10: 0-8069-8951-3

CONTENTS

INTRODUCTION

One question I'm often asked is how I come up with ideas for my crosswords. While my answer could be voluminous (or—as in my daughter's attempt to describe my hair on a humid day—"volumatic"), I'll give just a couple of examples from this book.

In some cases, I actively seek ideas. I'll run a current phrase through my mind to see how it might become the theme itself, rather than one of the entries in the puzzle. "Think Outside the Box" happened this way—the title came first, then I figured out how it could ... well, you'll see.

Other times, the ideas find me. Some years ago when my son and daughter, at ages 5 and 3, had been attempting headstands on some old couch cushions, Anna's hair was having serious fly-away problems. Jonathan looked at her and exclaimed "Her hair is full of ecstatic!" I knew that someday I'd try to work that into a crossword, and you'll find it here.

Of course the theme is only part of a puzzle. Slightly twisted clues such as the ones below can add to the fun of solving, whatever the theme may be.

Race that's always a tie? (ASCOT)
Cutlet? (NICK)
Perform a scull operation (ROW)

Most of the crosswords in this book have themes designed to elicit laughs (or groans!). I hope you have as much fun solving the puzzles as I did creating them.

—Cathy Allis Millhauser

UNSILENT PARTNERS

It's about time the other half has its say

ACROSS

1 Item that may be out of date?
4 Pack rat's collection
8 Muscle problem
13 Muscle problem
15 Jack Kent cartoon king
16 "Are you *listening*?"
17 What a waiter must do?
20 Awards for Lucci and Lahti
21 Be bearish
22 Have a hart
23 Boil
25 Exercise
27 Specialty bake shop chain?
34 Hearty partner
37 Tadpole's dad, maybe
38 Musteline swimmer
39 Fold lady
40 Clement
42 Pod opener

43 Dogie catcher
45 Kon-Tiki Museum site
46 Stable locks
47 Nerdy main squeeze?
50 Trojans' sch.
51 Torment
55 Intent look
58 Faraday named them
62 Friend of Mercutio
63 Scaffold?
66 Soft and smooth
67 Irish New Age singer
68 Diminutive suffix
69 Nursery rhyme veggie
70 Coming up

71 Peruvian money unit

DOWN

1 Turns wan
2 *It was vani* to Caesar
3 Mint family member
4 Wrench part
5 Brew holders
6 Quarter is one kind
7 Gerhard Schroeder's predecessor
8 Cable movie channel, for short
9 Refine
10 *Betsy's Wedding* director
11 Whole lot

12 Eve's counterpart
14 Susan Hayward's real first name
18 Org. concerned with ergonomics
19 Hebrew month
24 Folies-Bergère set/costume designer
26 ATM feature
28 Lifesaver, often
29 Parent
30 *Island of the Blue Dolphins* author
31 *A Bug's Life* princess
32 Kind of bar
33 Base for Oliver Hazard Perry

34 Steersman's post
35 Gone
36 End end
40 Singers Rawls and Reed
41 Linguist Chomsky
44 Needs oil, maybe
46 1973 Paul McCartney hit
48 Litmus paper reddener
49 *Cannery Row* character Flood
52 Issues
53 Take care of
54 Beach bag filler
55 Sound of one starting
56 "___ the Agent" (old comic strip)
57 Writer Émile
59 TV lawyer Marshall
60 Cardinal number?
61 "The Hateful" river
64 Deli choice
65 Jipijapa product

ANSWER, PAGE 82

I SWALLOWED SOME BEES!
Ouch!

ACROSS

1 First pope
6 Heeds a curve on scores
11 Respond to treatment
15 Ex of Rod and George
16 *Gulliver's Travels* creatures
18 Chorus girl, maybe
19 Marx brother running scared?
21 A ton
22 Cultivated
23 Item that might chip some teeth if eaten?
25 Dieter's undoing, often
28 Spare
29 Miss a spare
30 Pole, e.g.
33 Brook sound
35 Cerberus guarded it
37 Household spirits
39 Wet septet
40 Home, for Oscar the Grouch
41 Giants Hall of Famer
42 Conundrum

44 Bicycles built for two
48 Announcement at the oasis?
51 Like a Slinky
52 Solo
53 Forensic ID
54 Score half
55 Kind of chart
56 Tomorrow's T-bone
58 Euripedes drama
61 Emulated wind
63 Anent
64 Had shad
65 One of four-on-the-floor
67 Crest competitor
69 Ride in style?
72 Bare
76 Goodbye, Colombo

77 Get-together for low-rent types?
80 Made a touchdown
81 Certain whitemen
82 Result
83 Coops and cotes
84 *Divine Commedia* author
85 Service club members

DOWN

1 Covenant
2 Like some textbook publishers
3 End
4 Culture within another

5 Croupier's role
6 Its opp. is ant.
7 Stay back
8 Nope
9 Mythical twin
10 Actress Ellen
11 Way through school
12 Made a flight to unite
13 *Vogue* subject
14 Misfits
17 Biological body
20 Mount Hor's ancient land
24 Augments
26 Edible bivalve
27 Whirling
30 Arboreal hanger-on
31 Shaper in shop
32 Soviet cooperative
34 Sicilian wine

36 Painter Hiroshige
38 Post-Sputnik period
40 City on the Arno
43 Qaboos bin Said's realm
44 Gardening tool
45 German seaport
46 Tram rider, perhaps
47 A drum
49 Quote
50 Way to go
55 Preparation for babies
57 Some drums
58 Zany
59 Parisian star
60 Hold, in a way
61 Sent
62 Girls who want to have fawn?
66 Threat ender
68 Oust
70 Red ___ (candy brand)
71 It's a sign
73 Roughly
74 Knock for a loop
75 They move in orbits
78 Sgt. Baracus portrayer
79 Language suffix

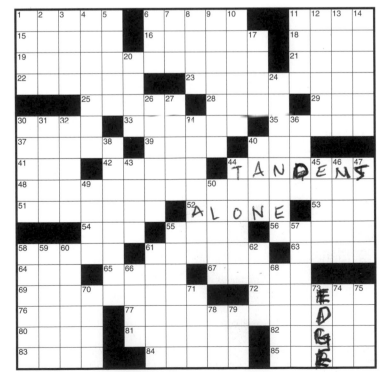

DOUBLE TAKES

Take your time

ACROSS

1 They come in chocolate
5 Undercoated
11 Military order: Abbr.
14 Hissed "Hey!"
18 Double-reed instrument
19 Von Trapp family song
20 Yesterday: French
22 Home of Loretta and Brigham Young
23 Take five?
25 *Splendor in the Grass* screenwriter
26 Hardly like Emily Post
27 Up ___ (cornered)
28 Explosive stuff
29 Take charge?
32 "Queen of Mean" Helmsley
33 Handel oratorio King
35 Christmas at the Vatican
36 Vote for
37 Twist
39 Palestrina piece
41 Stonewashed stuff
43 Biblical transport

45 Decide
48 Jackson Five member
49 Polishes off
51 Take stock?
56 Hall of Famer Byron
58 Astronaut's growth
59 Iris's eye layer
60 San Francisco's ___ Hill
62 Hibernia
63 Knowing, in a scientific name
65 Kaffiyeh wearer
68 Alkaline solutions
71 Big business big shot
72 Take issue?
76 Needing no Rx
79 One of the Pleiades
80 Pearl Harbor locale
81 In a distinguished way
85 *The Twits* author
87 Miró images
89 Alphabet quartet
91 It's for high living

92 Lindgren : Pippi :: Thompson : ___
95 Take cover?
99 *Limelight* allurer
101 Taylor in *Mystic Pizza*
102 English novelist Barbara
103 Camptown Races racer
104 Cubic meter
105 Furnish (with)
107 Perfunctory osculation
110 Take, perhaps
112 Shrewd
114 Poverty, figuratively
117 Father of "The Force"
120 Take the rap?
123 Legendary elephant devourer
124 Horseshoe-shaped hardware piece
125 Thesis protex
126 Approximately
127 Take turns?
130 Pizazz
131 Freshman, usually
132 Resident of Rennes, e.g.

133 *You've Got Mail* director Ephron
134 Take trains
135 Jimjams
136 Cremona creations, briefly
137 Maize mush

DOWN

1 Kind of color
2 Lessen
3 Take the cake?
4 Venus's sister
5 ASAP
6 Rummages about
7 Skater Rodnina
8 Chin, to anatomists
9 CPR giver, often
10 Course
11 Polanski hit film of 1974
12 *Monkeys* writer Susan
13 Shame
14 Utter
15 Take notes?
16 "Sexy ___" (Beatles song)
17 Iota preceder
21 Scrub over
24 Whale's gestation period
30 And ___ grow on

31 French income
34 Rake
38 1990s game-craze piece
40 Psychological wink
42 Michigan's ___ Royale
43 Messages re perps
44 Yankees' home from '74 to '75
46 Former European state
47 Hebrew letter
50 Sponge feature
52 Speaker on the diamond
53 Concert hall
54 Comice, for one
55 Vaughn's character in "The Man From U.N.C.L.E."
57 Paleo- opposite
61 Shortly
64 Atlanta Hawks' org.
66 Legal eagles' org.
67 Conduct
69 Comedian Philips
70 Beelzebub

73 Pop singer Vikki

74 Pipe

75 Went right, in oaters

76 Horace lines

77 Mohs scale softie

79 Take place?

82 Take a powder?

83 Film director Wertmuller

84 Human cracker

86 Enumerate

88 PBS fundraisers

90 Graduate topper

93 Lieu

94 Auditory range

96 Sal with a *Giant* role

97 Paleo-

98 Rogue

100 Called it a night

106 Media giant Time ___

108 Twelfth month of a certain calendar

109 Desi's compatriots

110 If Spooner were one, he'd sew you to your sheets

111 Pointed tools

113 Coup

115 More than wanna

116 Boston specialty

118 Dream ender

119 Backpack part

121 Zero

122 Industrial pollutants of EPA concern

128 Leftover for Rover

129 Carry-___ (small luggage)

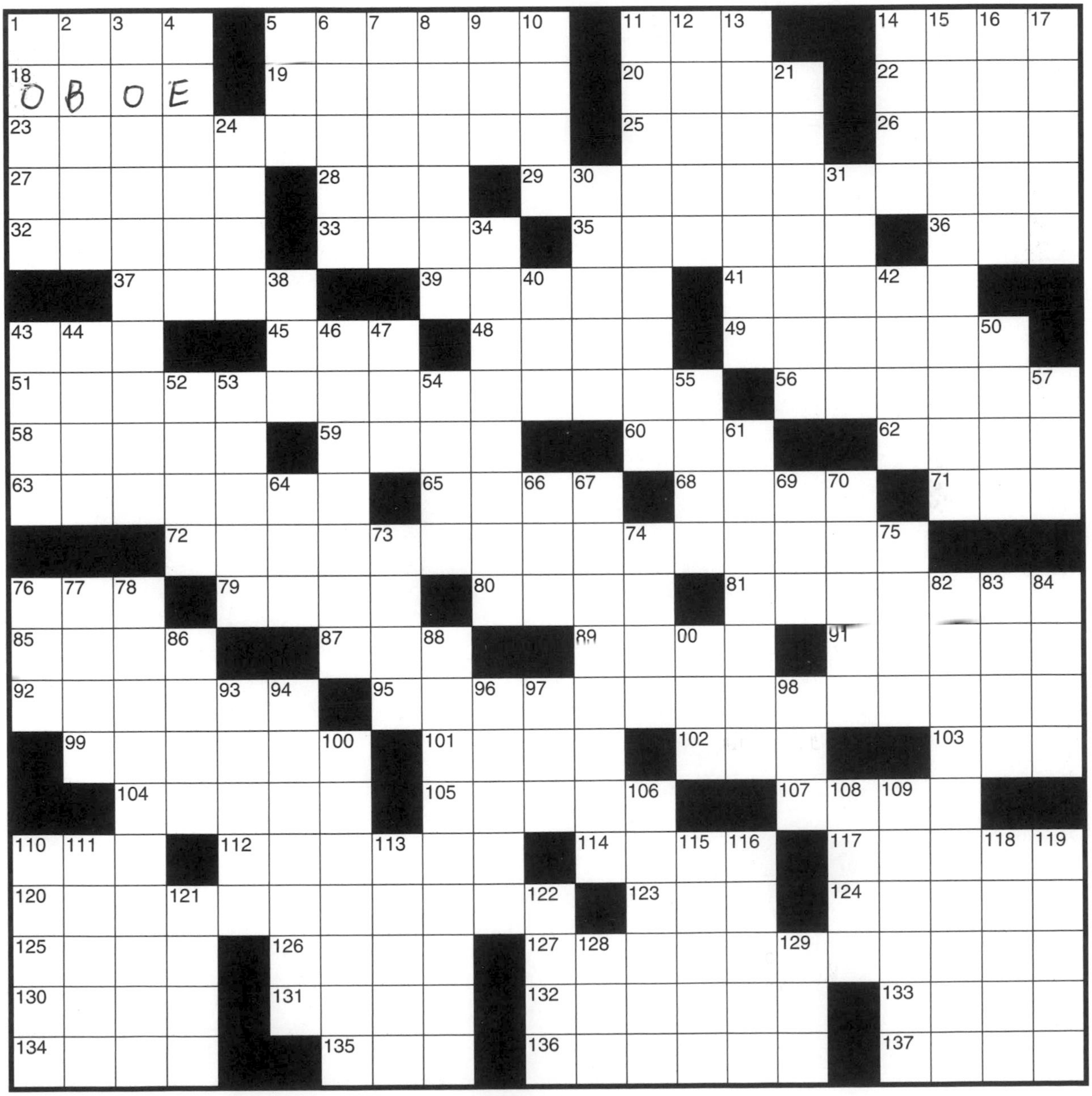

GYM DANDY
A workout sure to leave you groaning

ACROSS
1 Contribute to crime
5 Hotel home of Eloise
10 Spanakopita cheese
14 Secure with a clove hitch
15 Valleys
16 A lot of bulls
17 They sound like leg muscles with bad habits?
19 *Atlas Shrugged* author
20 What a prankster may be on
21 He loved Lucy
22 In addition
23 Secular
25 Hotel offerings
27 It sounds like a sniper's practice on back muscles?
32 Like Cheerios
33 Heche of 1998's *Psycho*
34 Take off a brooch

38 Spanish eye
39 NOW founder
41 French word in a cleanser brand
42 Singing Carpenter
44 Shticks
45 Cad's comeuppance
46 They sound like poorly outlined chest muscles?
49 Mount Everest guide
52 Media for Van Gogh
53 Hip joint
54 Armful, e.g.
58 Epithet
61 Lena in *Chocolat*

62 It sounds like the answer to stomach muscle problems?
64 Join
65 "Hi and Lois" twin
66 Kind of pricing
67 Cleaning solutions
68 It raises dough
69 Stationer's stuff

DOWN
1 Thomas ___ Edison
2 Jailbird's godsend
3 Story-to-story conveyor
4 Shrink rap?
5 Pronto, initially
6 Praise

7 Biological wings
8 Greek : omegas :: British : ___
9 St. Francis's birthplace
10 Like some affairs
11 Praise
12 It may be perfect
13 South American expanse
18 Pair on Hermann Maier
24 Type of room, nowadays
26 Word on many a penny
27 Lifted

28 Turbaned prince
29 Famed L.A. Laker
30 Chilling
31 Campsite sight
35 The Holy Land
36 Apple offering
37 Pinches
39 Shearing sound
40 It touted "the sign of extra service"
43 Gofer work
45 Call it quits
47 Ailment
48 In ___ (where originally placed)
49 Show disapproval
50 Like sponges
51 Banish
55 "Alice's Restaurant" officer
56 Famed terrier role
57 Fiji three
59 Chops choice
60 Tolkien tree creatures
63 Realtor's listing

ANSWER, PAGE 88

10

RUSH JOB
A special holiday blend

ACROSS

1 Humphrey Bogart topper
7 They're good to have met
12 Zilch, in Zaragoza
16 Player
17 Lane
18 Runner's circuit
19 Start of an original verse
22 Whiffenpoof singer, e.g.
23 Ken or Lena in acting
24 Dogie catcher
25 Wife of Saturn
27 One named
30 Kind of list
34 PDQ
37 ___ Verde National Park
38 Part 2 of the verse
44 Door word
45 Like barbecue coals, often
46 Jazz grp.
47 Ilk of Ananias
48 Seminar setting, perhaps
49 Floral essence
51 Furniture wood
52 Corsairs' conveyance
53 In ___ (instantly)
54 Part 3 of the verse
58 People go by it
59 Old ruler

60 Popular computer game series
61 Corporate climber's sine qua non
65 Alkali in cleansers
67 Wild thing
69 Part of SEATO
71 Chutney fruit
76 End of the verse
80 Diva's selection
81 Cheri of *Scary Movie*
82 Juiced
83 *Buddenbrooks* author
84 Lifeboat lifting device
85 Bebe ___ (friend of Richard Nixon)

DOWN

1 Sly
2 Humorist Bombeck
3 Often-knurled cylinder
4 Done: Prefix
5 Eloper of fiction
6 Actress Sue ___ Langdon
7 Stuff in kitchen chem. experiments
8 Precollege, for short
9 African antelope
10 Cozy wing, maybe
11 Barrett of Pink Floyd
12 Fragrant handheld?
13 Passerine or anserine, e.g.

14 Football Hall of Famer Lavelli
15 Sea lettuce and such
20 Martini's vermouth partner
21 O' men?
26 Hangs (around with)
28 Spam container
29 Religion division
30 Family including poplars
31 Eighth-century Hebrew prophet
32 "Calendar Girl" singer
33 Play that featured Diane Keaton
35 It needs free oxygen
36 Cover-up excuse

39 In medias ___
40 Opts
41 Thing
42 Adder that won't sting
43 Least well done
48 California or New Jersey's ___ Park
49 Words with standstill or glance
50 Quick cut
52 VI × VII
53 Skewed
55 Isolde's beloved
56 Starbucks offering
57 Finnish architect Alvar
61 At right angles to a keel
62 Stiller partner
63 Sink
64 Israeli desert region
66 Roast host
69 Kin of horti-
70 State of vexation
72 Starbuck's captain
73 "Little ___ in Slumberland" (classic comic)
74 Mild oath
75 Latin word on the Great Seal
77 Punishment symbol
78 Airport monitor info
79 Canine caveat

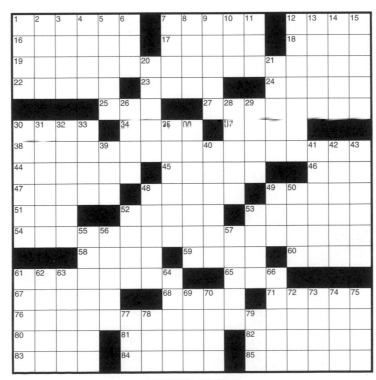

ANSWER, PAGE 90

11

TRIPLE FEATURE
In more ways than one

ACROSS

1 Spills the beans
6 Baby manatee
10 Graceful prancer
14 It may be liquid
15 Eye layer containing the iris
16 Make stew?
17 Hawaiian Punch fruit
18 No foe
19 Double-click target
20 Stanley Kubrick swan song film, 1999
23 Maid Marian : Olivia :: Robin Hood : ___
25 Intentionally cutting
26 Clings (to) or separates
28 Bathed on dry land
32 Clint Eastwood western, 1967
35 Carte lead-in
36 Duvet filling
37 Ending in commercial coinages
38 *Encino Man*'s Sean

40 Chemical compound suffix
41 Natural disaster film, 1988
43 Mother ___
46 Certain playing marble
47 ___ flask (thermos)
50 Miniature gulf?
51 What these theme films are, as a whole
55 Baylor University site
56 God of the Hindu trinity
57 Room mate?
61 Former Yemeni capital

62 ___-Neisse Line (Polish-German boundary)
63 Daytime Emmy winner Susan
64 Kind of sale
65 New Jersey sports team
66 Joel's brother and partner in filmmaking

DOWN

1 Diamond corner
2 Fighting Tigers' sch.
3 Simile center
4 Pop, but not Mom
5 Spend the night

6 What bears bear
7 Purports
8 Bolshevism founder
9 Like Beanie Babies
10 Sprung up
11 More than making ends meet
12 Noted baseball family name
13 Propensity
21 Adj. re a sch.
22 Net suffix re a sch.
23 Benjamin's beloved in *The Graduate*
24 Hand down
26 Swindler

27 Diner at "Roz's Roost"
29 Christmas, Italian-style
30 Draw forth
31 Author Alighieri, more familiarly
33 Quebec's ___ d'Orleans
34 Synapses and such
38 Open (to)
39 Explain in detail
41 Occurs to
42 Pack ___ (quit trying)
44 Oscar winner O'Brien
45 Lever half?
48 Whispered passage, perhaps
49 Seam strengthener
51 Like some conference calls
52 Early word
53 Hot cross buns crosser
54 Levers that work together
58 *Wein* wail
59 Co. touted by Nipper
60 Uproar

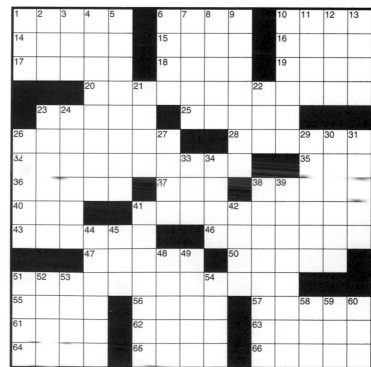

ANSWER, PAGE 92

SMALL CHANGE
Just don't fall asleep at the switch

ACROSS
1 Cold response
7 Hosts
10 Purim's month
14 Stinging insect pulp
15 Fashionable do
16 Sports victim of 1993
18 Boxing ring?
20 Pinch
21 Overcharge
22 Home of Millay and Longfellow
23 Slew, slangily
24 Why a lot of people saw *The Doctor*?
29 Course for U.S. newcomers
32 Henley crewmen
33 Heirs' inheritance
34 Shed
36 You can believe it
39 Dupes some wedding officiants?
45 Crumbs
46 Opera singer Nixon
47 Aiea's island
49 Washington senator getting carried away?
54 Like Harvard's walls
55 Dock workers
56 Hard to understand

60 Tours yours
62 Actor Stephen
63 Communication device way ahead of its time?
68 ___ *probandi* (burden of proof)
69 Ranch in Ferber's *Giant*
70 Contribute to crimes
74 Wickerwork willow
76 Where damaged projectors end up?
79 *The Gondoliers* girl
80 *Padre*'s brothers
81 Word's last syllable
82 Slumber

83 Cousin of "Rah!"
84 President nicknamed Old Rough and Ready

DOWN
1 Assumes a lotus position
2 Sound from Santa
3 Inventor's genesis
4 Pop singer Carr
5 Brian of Roxy music
6 Kind of room
7 *West Side Story* song
8 Trolley toll?
9 Foodstuff from orchids

10 Rebuker of Balaam
11 Gov. Clinton
12 Actress Silverstone
13 Seek absolution
15 Alums
17 Papyrus is one
19 Poet who was master of the ruba'i
25 Fast-food option
26 Nobel-winning chemist Otto
27 Enact anew
28 ___ now (at this point)
29 An Orr teammate, familiarly
30 Drinking sound
31 Kind of jackpot

35 Olympics boycotter of '84
36 Gave two hoots
37 Watermelon waste
38 Playwright Bogosian
40 Prefix with valence
41 Anemic-looking
42 Fictional Okie
43 Check writer
44 Sexuality writer Hite
48 Bruin, to Brutus
50 Do some frosting
51 French "with"
52 Stratagem
53 Lesson reader, in some churches
56 Brewing
57 Beautician role
58 Vacation at sea
59 Check out
60 GM or MG products
61 Song syllables
64 Sister of Euterpe
65 *On the Beach* author Shute
66 Western resort lake
67 Nuts
71 Help, with "out"
72 "Blondie" boy
73 Boyars' ruler
75 Stinker
77 Situate
78 Waterfront workers' org.

ANSWER, PAGE 94

BRIDGE CROSSINGS

An interview with an unusual couple

ACROSS

1 Jeers
7 Lena of *Romeo Is Bleeding*
11 Tub filler
15 Home of Iowa State
19 Won spender
20 Surrealist artist from Barcelona
21 Julie's *Dr. Zhivago* costar
22 Wilson's predecessor
23 Why are you always with Mrs. Bridge?
26 Effluvium
27 *Thumbelina* character
28 Part of a signature
29 More, in a score
30 Tray
32 Mrs. Bridge is very strong, no?
37 Postal workers, at times
40 Alt. to Pennzoil
41 Plus
42 Ridge on, say, a dial
43 Russian river
45 Tourist, to the Beatles
50 What would you call your relationship?
56 Make a graven image
57 Wock musician Barrett
58 Hawthorn's cousin
59 Character actor J. Carrol
61 Tournament big shot
62 Pulitzer poet Van Buyn
63 Betel palm's genus
65 Theater guides
67 Why is Mr. Bridge so fidgety?
72 Andy, TV's raspy-voiced "Jingles"
73 Platters
74 Locus
75 Enveloped by
76 Owen of silents
78 Ark. neighbor
79 Old hand
82 Kitchen "cubist"
84 What was Mrs. Bridge doing when you met?
89 In the courtroom hot seat
91 Been prone
92 *Psycho* setting
93 Feature of Dr. Dentons
96 It airs *ER*
97 With eyes wide open
99 What did you give Mr. Bridge?
105 Orkin target
106 *Domingo* is one
107 Dig like a pig
108 "Cogito ___ sum": Descartes
112 Like the Joker
113 Wasn't that a bit risky?
118 Dickensian orphan
119 Mare hair
120 Washstand item
121 Disengaged
122 Snake eyes topper
123 Part of BPOE
124 Rolls of dough
125 Hand down

DOWN

1 Milk choice
2 Gabrielle Chanel's nickname
3 Like some agreements
4 Small opening, in biology
5 Kind of "farm"
6 Hit man, maybe
7 Swiss watch company
8 Inspirits
9 Vexation
10 Postal Creed word
11 Humbert's beloved
12 Foreign affairs?
13 Appeared in print
14 Its drawers hold drawers
15 Under any circumstances
16 "The ___ Decade" (nickname of the 1890s)
17 Violinist Zimbalist
18 Long, hard look
24 Some have *the*
25 Likely
31 Room at the top
33 Tiller turner
34 Another, for Andalusians
35 ___ the crack of dawn
36 Jungian author Clarissa Pinkola ___
37 Riadou on a Street
38 "Walk ___" (Dionne Warwick hit)
39 Wished undone
44 Napery
46 Ottoman bigwig
47 Groom plumes
48 Tinker's target
49 First pro baseball team, today
51 Wraps up
52 Wife of *The Little Tramp* actor
53 Ramble
54 Prolific cantata composer
55 Go-between
60 Get a move on
63 Set at
64 Ocasek of the Cars
66 Javelin throwers, e.g.
67 Confine
68 Turn out

69 One who's "not It"
70 Elton John's "___ Dancer"
71 Certain Hindu
72 Pedestal part
77 Renown
79 Brad in *True Romance*
80 Film holder
81 Parisian hub
83 Gotten puffier, in a way
85 Anna Sten role of 1932
86 Any of the Bee Gees
87 Acquired, as a bill
88 Presages
90 Day or night
94 Generic small town
95 Biblical "hits"
97 Last name in chocolate chip cookies
98 Abates
99 16th-century council site
100 Emulate a hummingbird
101 Caesar was one
102 "Pogo" creator Walt
103 Barbasco's veggie cousin
104 Museum docent's responsibility
109 Pythagorean P's
110 Footballer Marchetti
111 Presage
114 Bud
115 Hemlock relative
116 It carried folks "up, up, and away"
117 Words before "while"

VANISHING POINTS
We love to see you smile

ACROSS
1 Justice Fortas
4 Boxcars, e.g.
8 Kind of palm
13 Romaine by another name
14 Neck of the woods
15 Singer called a "Latin Madonna"
16 Causing mortification
18 Jim Carrey was green for this role
19 Tchotchke
20 *The Fairie Queene* poet
21 "Mama" who sang with Phillips
23 Response to a backrub
24 Line on a spine
27 Sensational
29 Nice friend
32 Threat words
34 Reveille counterpart
35 Older shavers
36 Homer Simpson's watering hole

37 Makes finer, in a way
39 Hosp. staffers
40 Otorhinolaryn-gologist; Abbr.
41 The ears have it
42 Hepburn's costar in *The Lion in Winter*
44 A meaning of -y
45 Solitary type
47 "What ___!" ("Hilarious!")
48 Mrs. William McKinley
50 Dream up
52 Card trick?
55 Snoozes
59 State of wrath
60 Travel

61 Extent
62 Pointer's clue
63 Kind of feline
64 Chess mates?
65 Camera part
66 Use a crowbar

DOWN
1 Bank CD, e.g.
2 Nobel physicist Niels or son Aage
3 Actor Morales
4 Makes deeply resentful
5 Projecting window
6 Soup legume
7 Bring up the distant rear
8 Cuts short?
9 "Maria ___" (1963 hit song)

10 Dandruff sufferer's purchase, maybe
11 Depend end
12 He had a mane part?
15 Stuff on some dipsticks
17 Founders George (Audubon Society) and Josiah (college)
20 Cremona creation, briefly
22 Bested, say, the Cheshire Cat
24 Marisa in *What Women Want*
25 Monopoly tokens

26 Babies bite them
28 Jure or facto lead-in
30 ___ Park (Edison lab site)
31 Map feature
33 Switch suffix
38 Golf champion Els
39 Wagnerian title character
41 Sorts
43 Ragged clothing
46 Ebb
49 "Nothing runs like a ___"
51 *Titans* producer Spelling
52 Exit, à la the Cheshire Cat
53 ___ de Castro (Spanish noblewoman)
54 Salt Lake City-to-Provo dir.
56 *Modern Maturity* publisher
57 Feather prefix
58 Exciting, slangily
60 Cambodia's ___ Pot

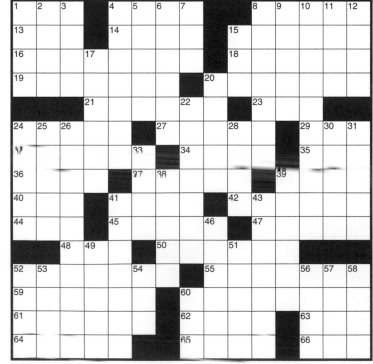

ANSWER, PAGE 82

YOU FIRST

Give it a chance before U-turn the page

ACROSS

1 Put up with
7 Bro's counterpart
10 Political interest group
14 Capacity
15 Reunion attendee, for short
17 Some confirmations
19 *Dallas* clan
21 Central Florida city
22 One-way ride?
23 Inedible cakes
24 Hyper
25 Ear's air pressure equalizer
29 Letter before beth
31 Orleans-to-Paris dir.
32 Flurry
33 Trunk
37 Miami, for one
41 Returnee's words
45 Coarse
47 Popi portrayer in film
48 Comedian Anne
49 Arrested, slangily
50 Catch some waves?
51 Like "plug-and-play" electronics
53 Dutch painter Jan

55 Key of Beethoven's *Emperor* concerto
56 Gamboling place
57 Leaf's main vein
59 Beaufort scale listings
61 Alaska neighbor
69 Hermitic
70 Herman's Hermits' Peter
71 Mint piece
75 Does macramé
76 "Rejoice in God," in Latin hymns
79 It's tossed at German restaurants
80 Hirobumi, Midori, and Lance

81 Mountain lion
82 Hockey's Phil, familiarly
83 Biblical suffix
84 Unattractive

DOWN

1 Greetings from Galba
2 Peach or Orange, e.g.
3 Bjorn loser?
4 Firth of Tay port
5 Med. test for muscle problems
6 "Awesome!" equivalent
7 Pago Pago's place
8 Of a pelvic bone
9 Prefix for an odorous element

10 Less rare, maybe
11 Permitted
12 Japanese industrial city
13 Little star?
16 Lanvin fragrance of yore
18 "Smooth Operator" singer
20 Halifax clock setting: Abbr.
26 Pulitzer winner Sinclair
27 Cry to a fly
28 Part of A.M.
29 More than likes
30 Behold
32 Maid in India
34 Lens holders
35 Hoskins's role in *Hook*
36 Where planes stop near Des Plaines

38 Mostly Muslim nation
39 Wad
40 Officials à la Caesar
42 Engage
43 *Carmina Burana* composer
44 Crumbly earth
46 "Orinoco Flow" singer
49 Do some roadwork
51 Hand or foot, e.g.
52 Parrot in Disney's *Aladdin*
54 Carmaker Maserati
58 Pooch in '70s films
60 Public lecture hall
61 Schmoozes
62 Radii companions
63 Alternative to Salems
64 Ready for drafting
65 Way to go
66 Artoo, for one
67 *The Secret of Roan ___* (1994 film)
68 # on forms
72 Sharpness
73 Patricia in 1993's *Heidi*
74 Loyalist
77 "Woe!" in Worms
78 Superfluously

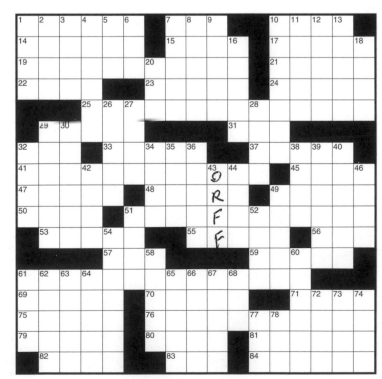

ANSWER, PAGE 84

BOARD GAME
Sort of a 2 × 8 construction

ACROSS

1 Son of Isaac and Rebecca
5 Handheld helper, briefly
8 Kind of money or bomb
13 1960s-fest
14 *New Yorker* cartoonist Peter
16 Small drum
17 BOARD TYPE, BOARD TYPE (mattress support)
19 A bout place
20 Bout
21 BOARD TYPE, BOARD TYPE (fastener)
23 Time Warner "pard" since 2001
25 Biological protuberance
26 BOARD TYPE, BOARD TYPE (aftermath)
31 Oman's capital
35 Wings
36 Poison control substance
38 Actress Dolores Del ___
39 Figurative moments
41 Acapulco gold
42 Stand on a street corner
44 Sellout abbr.
45 Apprentice
48 Popular pop
49 With 9-Down, Philippine also known as "The Iron Butterfly"
51 BOARD TYPE, BOARD TYPE (pre-rollerblade gizmo)
53 ___-de-boeuf (oval window)
55 Domino dot
56 BOARD TYPE, BOARD TYPE (certain Algonquian)
61 Bob Fosse's field
65 Talk show host Lake
66 BOARD TYPE, BOARD TYPE (tally sheet)
68 Caper
69 Blackjack dealer's device
70 Genuflection juncture
71 Smooth-scaled lizard
72 ___ Betsy (Crockett's rifle)
73 Strewn

DOWN

1 Flows back
2 Flow slowly (through)
3 Home-care worker
4 Awaiting allaying
5 Excellence lead-in
6 Kind of grind
7 Magnani or Paquin
8 BOARD TYPE, BOARD TYPE (Pequod first mate)
9 See 49-Across
10 Explorer Tasman
11 Pasta ___ (Quaker Oats brand)
12 Slangy mouth
15 Russ. secret police, 1924–34
18 Do some tilling
22 1996 Gwyneth Paltrow film
24 Vietnam War's My ___ incident
26 Their voices are *profundi*
27 Cause quaking
28 Its paddlings don't hurt
29 Spy
30 Contraction from Ed McMahon
32 Swindler
33 Usher's beat
34 Hungarian wine
37 Stopper
40 BOARD TYPE, BOARD TYPE (alter ego)
43 Treatments for swelling
46 Ingenue
47 Afternoon treat, maybe
50 Commit to, as a price rate
52 Current or trend
54 Insurance company concern
56 Cup holders?
57 Internet connector
58 Opera opening
59 *Pulpo*'s arm-count
60 Hardware store buy
62 One billionth: Prefix
63 Hands
64 Churchill successor
67 Roulette bet

ANSWER, PAGE 86

IT HAPPENS WHEN ...

You *can* have it both ways

ACROSS

1 Is no good, slangily
7 Capital of Rwanda
13 Kin of "Bobby Hockey"
17 Royal robe trim
18 Globular flute
20 Twofold
21 ... Spot gently paws Bert and Ernie
23 Tennis player Roddick
24 ___ Maria (Jamaican liqueur)
25 Flagellum
26 Expressions akin to "Obviously!"
28 Sweep
29 Maine's ___ au Haut
31 Tableland
34 Mark down
36 ... baboons are put through the paces by their owner
41 Former California fort
42 Its acad. is in Colorado Springs
43 Where many llamas range
44 ... a teen's room has a posting of Sassoon and such
51 Schlocky
52 Roars for some Lions
53 Half of a potato brand
54 Diamond Head locale
58 MSN alternative
59 Lizard-like
61 Pipsqueak

63 Au ___ (served like prime rib)
64 Heelless slipper
66 Well suited
67 Taken in, in a way
68 Busy American hub
70 ... fortifications are split in two by a beam
74 Worm portal, perhaps
77 Neither masc. nor fem.
78 Stir-fry cookery need
79 ... a *Sopranos* star catches small birds
86 Turn signal, e.g.
87 Have a hunch
88 Gets paid to care
90 Golf champ Ernie
91 Publisher of *My Generation*
93 Kind of jerk
96 Goat quote
97 Drink trademark since 1945

99 ... bull's-eyes are made by a seafarer
104 Round holder?
105 Squealer
106 A pinniped carnivore
107 Bit of Scotch on New Year's Eve?
108 Put side by side
109 Like enamel finishes

DOWN

1 Cal. page starter
2 Platitude
3 Long-time Chevrolet model
4 Don't quite bite
5 "Who ___?"
6 *Wagon Train*'s Major Adams
7 Host of *Nightline*
8 ER discharge site
9 Old Navy affiliate, with "The"
10 *Human Concretion* sculptor
11 *Schwan* song

12 Singly and sequentially
13 Harem room
14 Go on a rampage
15 Rudimentary root
16 Slicker's trait
19 Incinerated
22 ___ Valley (Reagan Library site)
27 Platter licker of rhyme
30 Name on a famed B-29
32 Resembling a Sno-Cone
33 Helpers: Abbr.
35 Erstwhile detergent
37 Problems for insomniacs
38 Short courses?
39 Nichols's comedy partner
40 Blooming
44 Shell game
45 It once preceded "art"

46 Attention-getter
47 Stowe, Vermont's ___ Family Lodge
48 Leaping
49 Grantorto's *Faerie Queene* victim
50 Yule in the pulpit: Abbr.
55 A bit cracked
56 Mar
57 Implements
60 Machinery wheel
61 Seeds' hard integuments
62 Visit briefly
65 Burdon and Clapton
67 Nonsense partner
69 Forces to go
71 Hilo hello
72 Legal matter
73 Low
74 Belongings
75 Irvine's Everest fellow-climber
76 Aleut, e.g.
80 ___-foot oil
81 Correction section
82 Tenant
83 Heparin target
84 Official race requirements
85 Ranking
89 Pert
92 Tent stake, e.g.
94 "Deputy ___" (cartoon character)
95 Inland Asian sea
98 It may be electric
100 DDE's party
101 *Xanadu* grp.
102 Frank McCourt memoir
103 Day-___ paint

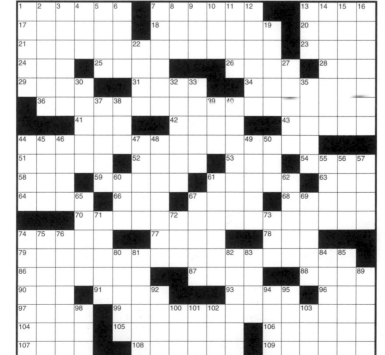

ANSWER, PAGE 88

CUTESY

Now, see here ...

ACROSS

1 Celesteville's king
6 Meal ground from maize
10 Sinking-feeling expression
14 Dwelling
15 ___ Sultan (Rimsky-Korsakov character)
16 Not "for here"
17 What one who has bowed to a lady might do?
20 More than close
21 Prizms, Storms, etc.
22 Atlas feature
23 Girl in *The Clan of the Cave Bear*
25 Part of NEA
27 Reading for Thumbelina?
33 Winged
34 Trini's *Little Women* role
35 Call a sinner thinner?
37 Favorite
38 Afforded a second engagement
42 Div. of Verizon
43 Cold-shoulder
45 Schmatte
46 *Barbarella* actor Milo
48 Goat's scapegoat?
52 Belgian songwriter Jacques
53 Shakespearean "demi-devil"
54 Latin for "elsewhere"
57 Drying kiln
59 Overwhelming defeat
63 Cease printing a Harold Robbins novel?
66 Emmy winner Falco
67 "Don't look ___!" ("I'm innocent!")
68 Like some of the Hebrides
69 Costly
70 General ___ chicken (Chinese entree)
71 Future fungus

DOWN

1 Diamond bases
2 Brother of Seth
3 Spanish wine sack
4 Unyielding
5 Camcorder abbr.
6 Trout hangout
7 Regarding
8 Muscle-soothing device
9 Get a hubcap (off)
10 Piece of cutlery
11 Stuff in stout
12 Scandalous scan
13 Hall of Fame pitcher Waite
18 Disagreeable
19 Swiss hotelier Cesar
24 Belgian North Sea feeder
26 Road hazard?
27 Lights-out signal
28 Greta Garbo, in *The Temptress*
29 "Mangia!"
30 Friend, to Francisco
31 Prime time time
32 First name in cosmetics
36 Bottom-heavy fruit
39 Celtic tongue
40 Barn areas
41 Magician Henning
44 Baby, at times
47 Accumulate for later
49 The Andrews Sisters, e.g.
50 Trawls
51 Subside
54 Passed, and then some
55 Burden (with)
56 Gold medal skater Kulik
58 Sphere head?
60 "The Iron Chancellor" Bismarck
61 One who's off the wagon
62 Lorry part
64 Like Easy Street's city?
65 Cattle genus

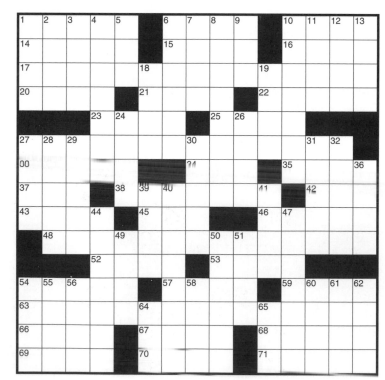

ANSWER, PAGE 90

OVER THERE
You'll soon know where

ACROSS

1 Margarine brand
7 Stand at ceremonies
11 Short form
15 How seashells get washed
16 Deterrent to productivity
18 Iago's *Era la notte*, for one
19 Girl in a Beach Boys song
20 Small fries?
22 Hibernation location
23 Wallaby's kin
25 Yummy, in some brands' spellings
26 Place with a very short lease?
31 Driver's lic. and such
32 Bossy on milk tins
33 Frames for, say, displays
35 Drive
38 Agile despite aging
40 Fix up a handyman special
43 Cells that fire
46 Mine, in Marseilles
48 Get board
49 Franken, Yankovic, etc.
50 What high-rise dwellers must do?
53 Tube stop, briefly
54 Crisps, e.g.

56 Lawyer Perry's creator
57 Butler's assistant, maybe
59 Acronym for an early computer
61 The Emerald Isle
63 Lightens
64 Girl group
66 *Eating* ___ (1982 cult comedy)
69 Horse-gambling spot, initially
71 Bangs on someone round the bend?
76 Pig, when truffle-hunting
78 "Miss Peaches" James of jazz
79 Quaker ___! (cereal name)

80 Sir Charles Percy's means of communication?
83 Scholarship surname
86 Hip about
87 Excelled
88 Home of the Green Wave
89 Famed Highlands lake
90 Southwestern plateau
91 Salmonoid fishes

DOWN

1 *Saturday Night Live* announcer
2 Wan
3 Gulf of Lion feeder
4 ___-*Tiki*
5 Dull finish?
6 Longs

7 Strips of rank
8 Licorice-like flavoring
9 Business abbr.
10 California's Big ___
11 Expressions of relief
12 Basis of this puzzle's theme
13 Human, e.g.
14 Levels, in Liverpool
17 Bits
21 Get paid for serving dinner
24 Nice answer?
27 Painter Jan van der ___
28 Think ___ (view disapprovingly)
29 Physicist Enrico
30 Downsizing move

34 Was a chair
35 Senseless
36 Sweet gourd
37 Pet interfering with loading up cars?
39 More wan
41 Door-flanking columns
42 Mexican side dish
44 Dunoon denial
45 Type of test
47 "Trial of the century" judge
51 "I Still See ___" (*Paint Your Wagon* song)
52 *Frère* counterpart
55 Japanese "yes"
58 Anklebones
60 Person in pics
62 Ethiopia neighbor
65 Permanent results?
67 Behave
68 Words on degrees
69 Welles of *The Third Man*
70 1,000 kilograms
72 *YM* readers
73 Of a protuberance
74 War of 1812 treaty site
75 Sussex trio
77 Terrible stage
81 Electrical resistance unit
82 Misery
84 Fan sound
85 Spanish fan's sound

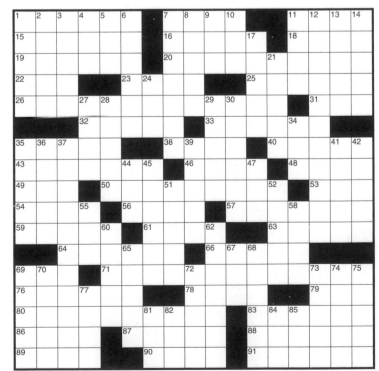

ANSWER, PAGE 92

NONVERBAL

This will have you seeing *things* right from the start

ACROSS

1 Information bit
6 Hankering
10 Hot dog topping
15 Designer Gucci
19 The accused's excuse
20 Writer Ephron
21 Brew type
22 Prepared to drive
23 What a bouncer might eat?
26 Corner of a diamond
27 Furrow maker
28 Class clown
29 Ewoks' moon
30 Prepares a drive
31 Wax, old-style
32 Top of a cathedral?
33 Shifts
34 Grounds for a bakery shoplifting charge?
40 Penn, in NYC
41 Penn State branch site
42 Straight, to mixologists
43 Rope on a ranch

45 Reason to hole up in one's room during a party?
52 Rock finale?
55 Most cunning
56 Tamblyn of *West Side Story*
57 Table
58 Singer Easton
60 ___-Lay
62 California wine county
63 "Am ___ blame?"
64 Reason for a collapse in a boudoir?
68 FedEx alternative
69 Whacked
71 Kind of accent
72 Mystery writing awards
74 Preacher on Mt. Sinai
75 *The Plague* setting
76 Politicians' concerns ...
78 ... and a slant used to help them
79 Result of shoddy workmanship at a stadium?
85 Model Campbell

87 Wedding ring?
88 '50s Hungarian premier Nagy
89 Young 38-Down
91 What you might see at a country tavern?
98 Hall of Famer Lou
100 Eclair finishers
101 Violinist Leopold
102 New on the job
103 Dwight's two-time rival
104 Defeat
106 Certain cross
109 Silent
110 Unlikely delivery to a tannery?
113 Month after Av
114 Like neon
115 Buggy place?
116 Stir
117 Birds' beaks
118 Traitor
119 Winter fender-bender cause
120 Playful animal

DOWN

1 T, in Morse code
2 Can for canines
3 Cause to yawn
4 Where, at the Forum
5 Hashes
6 It may be under a tongue
7 Vegan protein source
8 Do some photo editing
9 Ralph Kramden laugh syllable
10 Walker and Eastwood
11 *Messiah* composer
12 Slight, in a way
13 Glance askance
14 Verb type: Abbr.
15 Up
16 Part of a butterfly's snack routine?
17 Mojave, e.g.
18 Port of the *Potemkin* mutiny
24 Know-it-all
25 Believers such as Thomas Paine

30 Prayer
31 John of Monty Python
32 Catty
33 Some prayers, briefly
34 Abbr. on a VCR
35 Esposito teammate
36 Go flat?
37 John Lennon's in-laws
38 Salamander
39 Messes up
44 Student driver, probably
46 West Point frosh
47 Church council
48 Negotiate
49 Hackneyed
50 Detroit product
51 "Time ___ the essence"
53 Short-term staff
54 Times with significance
57 Gets away from
58 Condescend
59 Home brewery feature?

60 Establish
61 Dirt path feature
62 Papyrus is one
63 Oft-cloned PCs
65 Scarlett's plantation
66 Checkout counter procedure

67 Noodle
70 Ex-secretary Federico
73 More wan
75 Ear-related
76 Cross inscription
77 Lament
79 Complacent
80 Arab bigwig
81 Impressed expressions

82 Diplomat's place: Abbr.
83 Palindromic constellation
84 German article
86 Sleipnir's rider
89 Poultry farm workers
90 Rod used on the knuckles
92 Joshed

93 Eye layer
94 Animals
95 Moved quickly
96 Fanny
97 Prefix with sexuality
99 Bobbins
103 Japanese native
104 *The Caine Mutiny* author

105 Old Dodge
106 ___ *de suite* (all at once)
107 Cathedral projection
108 Netizen, e.g.
110 After-G string
111 Arteries with shoulders: Abbr.
112 Fold-up bed

ANSWER, PAGE 94

GIMME A LIFT
Featuring ways we raise

ACROSS
1 Freebie ticket, e.g.
5 Engine type
10 Do finish
14 Winds member
15 Berry in *X-Men*
16 Bath cooler
17 Derrick's place at night?
19 Gridiron group
20 Baffled
21 Often-yellow wheels
22 Loaf
23 Vex
25 City southwest of Le Havre
27 Tar's davit?
33 BP rival
36 They might be a round
37 Emmy winner Ed
38 Abbr. on Nova Scotia skeds
39 Less spare
41 Sch. founded by Thomas Jefferson
42 Union demand

44 Turgenev birthplace
45 Ear clearer
46 Block and tackle deliverer's shout?
49 Any one of HOMES
50 Books and people have them
54 Shock
56 Endangered goose
60 Military history's ___ *Gay*
61 Better *Better Homes and Garden*
62 Width of some windlasses?

64 Drum accompaniment
65 Baseball's "Hammerin' Hank"
66 *Uno*, in *TIm*
67 Slop
68 River winding through Idaho
69 Visit

DOWN
1 "Yankee Doodle Dandy" songwriter
2 Amin successor in 1980
3 Damp
4 Bread changed with centimos
5 Pen or hen, e.g.
6 Personal pie

7 Island near Capri
8 Rock Drummer Van Halen
9 Doc
10 Eternal
11 Kind of quick bread
12 City of central Poland
13 Besides
18 It's softer than gypsum
24 Part of QEF
26 From ___ (distant)
28 Distant
29 Surgery or motor starter
30 What -ate may mean, chemically

31 Son of Jacob
32 Drain part
33 Instrument for a Marx
34 Twin of Jacob
35 Many a Cezanne
39 Try for
40 Bridge expert Culbertson and others
43 Louvered
45 Preserve fruits
47 Rumormongers
48 Store sign
51 Well-pitched, perhaps
52 Verdugo of *Marcus Welby, M.D.*
53 Back-talking
54 Comic strip shorty of yore
55 "Garfield" growler
57 One who played Obi-Wan
58 Myrna, in *The Thin Man*
59 Fuzzy Endor denizen
63 Serpent's tail?

ANSWER, PAGE 96

UNMIXED VEGETABLES
Sufferin' succotash!

ACROSS

1 Madeline bared hers
5 O'Neill title trees
9 Edge (toward)
14 Circle dance
15 Spree
16 Hit with a joint
17 Portent
18 Versatile Japanese veggie?
20 Angular velocity symbol
22 Neck and neck
23 Houston in history
24 Choice veggie?
28 Feast
29 Pried without a lever
33 Docs who deliver
36 Kind of drive
38 End of an Oliver Twist request
39 Global veggie site?
44 Raced
45 Dr. ___ (Ming-Na's *ER* character)

46 Nonverbal "For shame!"
47 Color symbol for sin
51 Once-yoked folks
53 Hellish veggie-hauling job?
58 Greek 23rd
61 Race: Prefix
62 Country on the Gulf of Aden
63 Veggie guy in oaters?
67 *Sud* opposite
68 Arty gathering
69 With 60-Down, actor in Monty Python films
70 So

71 Go on a spree, maybe
72 City on the Truckee
73 E-mail command

DOWN

1 Prepared, say, James Bond's martini
2 Pre-clause pause
3 Doing a pirouette
4 Varied
5 Airport monitor abbr.
6 Powell's costar in *The Thin Man*
7 Carlo or Cristo lead-in

8 Flight segments
9 "23" follower in old slang
10 Ltd. counterpart
11 Mars, for one
12 Mother of Castor and Pollux
13 Mount Hor place of yore
19 Hessian possessive
21 Out of the way
25 Part of BTU
26 It's tender in Chile
27 Gambol
30 Pound was one
31 History chapters

32 Secretary, e.g.
33 Elects
34 Lobbying group
35 1986 Starship hit
37 Biz of "The Colonel"
40 Seuss zoo creature
41 Those guys
42 Half of dodeca-
43 Foe
48 Believe it or not
49 Steady
50 Flint-and-steel target
52 Opium, Obsession, etc.
54 France's longest river
55 Passion for Italians
56 Summer show
57 Over
58 Football move
59 Football move
60 See 69 Across
64 Those there
65 Sauterne, e.g.
66 Writer Umberto

ANSWER, PAGE 82

25

DIVISION OF LABOR
Some things never change

ACROSS
1 Paten place
6 Renoir contemporary
11 Official dismissal
18 Rouen's river
19 Banishment
20 Barbershop quartet song girl
21 Beaver State capital
22 Boring tool
23 Arnaz's *I Love Lucy* role
24 Start of a quote
27 It may hold a spray
28 What Sales pitched
29 Bow under pressure
32 Glide showily
36 Dinner rooster
39 Lily of the valley's shape
40 Virus medium, often
41 Part 2 of the quote
45 Latin I verb
46 Like some dementia
47 "Aye, aye" accompaniers
48 Author of the quote
50 Mythical giants
51 "Verrry interesting" Johnson
52 *Raison d'___*

54 As yet
58 Part 3 of the quote
65 Rhododendron species
67 Iago's wife
68 Father of Thor
69 Part 4 of the quote
71 Proportion let in
72 Last of the Stuart monarchs
73 A microscopy dye
74 Night light site
75 Court matter
76 Slightest utterance
78 Singer Mitchell
80 End of the quote
88 Head south, maybe
91 Way to read
92 Oar fulcrum
93 Property transferee
94 Material used for veils
95 Like a loon's cry
96 Howitzers, e.g.
97 City north of Salt Lake City
98 Friars Club event

DOWN
1 Prof. rank
2 Roy Orbison hit song
3 Domino, e.g.
4 Over
5 Meaning of "-ectomy"
6 Gives people hands
7 Radiate
8 Lerner and Loewe classic
9 Molson offerings
10 Fief worker
11 *Peter Pan* clan
12 Position held by Caesar
13 Rio Grande feeder
14 Norway's patron
15 Hitchcock title
16 Plus
17 Bert Lahr's sign, aptly
25 A skate is one
26 Put ___ (victimized)
29 They divide noses

30 Burns's partner
31 She played Cagney on TV
32 Brand
33 Magazine content, for short
34 Carmaker of the 9-5
35 Reporter on female sexuality
36 History Muse
37 Shakespeare title start
38 Painter Mondrian
39 Spell
41 What a shuttle carries
42 Concerning
43 Native land, to Livy
44 Senior Saarinen
46 Marble marking
49 Marker
52 Elver's elders
53 Jerk
54 Turkic language
55 Ultraviolet radiation absorber

56 Auroras
57 Lily family member
58 Dates
59 Katz of *Dallas*
60 Personal air
61 Boor
62 Joss, e.g.
63 Red-eye period, informally
64 Flier that makes one smart
66 Heinz Field footballers
70 Pueblo dweller
71 "Uncle!" crier
74 Atomic number of hydrogen
76 Kind of bar
77 "Daniel" singer
78 Unit of energy
79 Ancient
80 Common songbird
81 Brussels-based org.
82 Drink-downing sound
83 Informed
84 Godhead?
85 Dance at bar mitzvahs
86 Some Bulldogs
87 Comply with
88 Gaelic "son"
89 Dock workers' grp.
90 Tom Collins ingredient

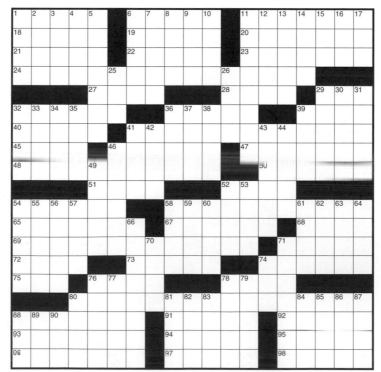

26

ANSWER, PAGE 84

HORSING AROUND
Horse laughs may ensue

ACROSS
1 List of duties
5 Bingo alternative
10 Gait trait
14 Folk singer/ activist Phil
15 Minimums for meetings
17 Finish line, often
18 Words overheard about the Old Gray Mare?
20 Dog food plugged by a Hoss
21 Richards of *Jurassic Park*
22 Horse head?
24 With 68-Across, circuit rider's task?
27 Agave fiber
28 Very, in Vichy
30 They have sub roles
34 Confuse
39 With 56-Across, power horse?
43 *Sum* translation
44 Australian lass
46 Major Baltic port
47 ___ avis
48 Apple-loving horse?
52 One Algonquian language
53 Nifty
54 Narrow-minded teacher

55 Half of a cleanser brand
56 See 39-Across
59 Picante
60 Dating from birth
62 Part of GRE
64 It's the pits
68 See 24-Across
74 Hypodermic, to some horses?
78 Nomad
79 Mustang sound, maybe
80 Where one might find a horse pill?
83 Fit
84 Removed, as notepad paper
85 Jumps the gun, e.g.
86 Southwest horizon hump

87 Went to court?
88 Condé in publishing history

DOWN
1 Painter Bonheur and activist Parks
2 Dark yellow color: Var.
3 His and her
4 State of northeast India
5 Film director Jean ___ Godard
6 Response to juicy news
7 Prop for Wile E. Coyote
8 Seaport near ancient Carthage

9 Certain sultanate native
10 Roan home
11 *Black Beauty*, for one
12 Baseball Hall of Famer Rixey
13 Drudge
15 Mod designer Mary
16 Some NCOs
19 Word with Cat or Cone
23 Apt for a horse's diet
25 Sun or moon
26 Org. that funds creators
29 Uncanny
31 Sporty Mazdas
32 Bring up
33 Wise guy
34 Prendergast's school of art

35 Jenna Elfman TV role
36 Fraud
37 Common teenspeak word
38 Jodie Foster was one
40 Personal quirk
41 I, to Claudius
42 Way off the highway
45 Egyptian cross
47 Kind of awakening
49 Sympathy partner
50 "Jingle Bells" contraction
51 Dispenser candy
56 Fan sound
57 Three-digit bus. number
58 Fan sound
61 Doria that sank
63 Warrant
65 End of a Nike ad slogan
66 "You're telling me!"
67 Clothing style
69 Slip-on shoe, for short
70 Made from a hardwood
71 Shadow
72 Moves in on
73 Meeting of lovebirds
74 Net user's nuisance
75 Bronchus, e.g.
76 Some include http
77 Starter for stat
81 Job ad abbr.
82 South of France

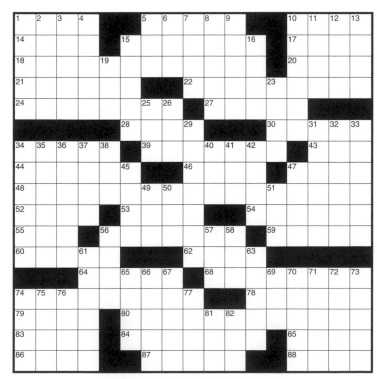

ANSWER, PAGE 86

27

TAKE IT WITH A GRAIN OF SALT

There's some symbolism herein

ACROSS

1 Buck
5 Thick piece
9 It may be hard
14 Wife of Zeus
15 Game divided into chukkers
16 Saw
17 "You said it!"
18 Corporate symbol
19 Stocking stuff
20 Farmer's restraints?
23 Uncut
24 Mideast carrier
25 Name of two Bible books
28 Keeping up (with)
32 *Bier* holder
35 Comparable
37 Final answer of bachelorhood
38 Mountain greenery?

42 Tristan-Isolde link
43 Hit a branch, maybe
44 *Now We Are Six* creator
45 The "Kum" in Kara Kum
48 "Time-out" behaviors
50 Lamb-like
52 Genetic engineering concern
56 Walk on oceanside rocks?
60 Composer Kurt
61 Caesarean salutations
62 Edit menu option
63 Little wet arm

64 James of *Murder By Death*
65 Whopper maker
66 Put a damper on: Var.
67 Lipinski rival in 1998
68 Abbr. in snail mail, but not e-mail

DOWN

1 Irritate
2 Genève's lake
3 Don't live
4 Window figure
5 Blood reservoir in the body
6 Its fruit is high in fiber
7 Kelp, for one

8 *Ain't That a Shame* singer
9 Cole Porter musical
10 Makeup of Virgil's *Bucolica*
11 Buttermilk's rider
12 Deterrents to teamwork
13 Erstwhile Nickelodeon toon
21 Skater Slutskaya
22 Sheath alternative
26 Vex
27 Airborne gaggle
29 Do something harrowing?
30 First place

31 Prepare to be shot
32 Eyed veggie
33 Pie crust holer
34 Winds up
36 Psyched about
39 Serve eats for bread
40 Chew the scenery
41 Seconds, maybe
46 Badge
47 Lots and more
49 Riddle with a baton
51 Flair
53 Ancient Asia Minor area
54 Musical *fini*
55 Put in, say, a magazine
56 Short guy?
57 Hair type
58 Profess
59 Intestinal pouches
60 Ill. neighbor

ANSWER, PAGE 88

ANIMAL TRAILS

Highway warnings that could be taken literally

ACROSS
1 Crude group?
5 *Beau* ___
10 Warner ___
14 Author Ephron
15 Transplant a plant
16 "Stupid me!"
17 Highway caution for eels?
20 Heptad plus one
21 Orgs.
22 Eisenhower and Turner
24 Beatles' meter maid
26 Highway cautions for fish?
33 Actress Dunne
34 Pull a coup d'etat
35 "It must be him ___ shall ..."
36 Baxter and Bundy
37 Tapestry city

38 Street, especially a "main" one
39 Use a +
40 Cry to *der Führer*
41 Command to Rover
42 Highway caution for centipedes?
46 Assails, with "into"
47 White-tailed eagle
48 Word on a "Wanted" poster
51 ___ in the bucket
54 Highway caution for asps?

60 Other: Spanish
61 Painter's prop
62 Haunted house sounds
63 Spotted
64 Part of LSU
65 Nancy of Carolyn Keene stories

DOWN
1 Switch settings
2 Water sport
3 ___ the Red
4 Under-lines?
5 Humperdinck heroine
6 Eternally, poetically
7 007, for one
8 Tote by boat
9 Biblical verb ending

10 Tree-trimming, Japanese-style
11 Corn ___ (African hairdo)
12 Word with season or sesame
13 Concordes
18 Tea type
19 Snacks
23 Game "keepers"?
24 1937 Eleanor Powell role
25 Advocates: Suffix
26 Ravi Shankar's instrument
27 Literally, "I believe"
28 Ibsen's Gabler

29 Reputed founder of Russia
30 Up, on a Spanish compass
31 Prayer before fare
32 Rifle attachment
37 ___, skip, and a jump
38 Put off
41 Dish for dippers: Var.
43 Puff of song
44 Sapient
45 Seer
48 Stirs
49 After midnight
50 About
52 Atop
53 Tiny dog, in slang
55 The thing, in law
56 Kind of meal
57 Gannett's ___ *Today*
58 Match part
59 Opposite of NNE

ANSWER, PAGE 90

OLDIES

Co-constructed with Terry Hackett

Have fun, boomers!

ACROSS

1 Mars
6 Tide type
10 Extra feature
15 EPA concern
19 Kind of symmetry
20 River of Northern Spain
21 Word on some egg cartons
22 One-fifth of CCXXX
23 5th Dimension lament for the bride's parents?
26 Nuisance
27 1973 Woody Allen hit
28 Arizona governor Jane ___ Hull
29 Beach Boys tribute to a growing waistline?
31 Groucho role B. Driftwood
33 Monogram of Garfield's successor
35 Gives lip to
36 Trouble
40 All worked up
44 Sticks in *The Color of Money*
45 Hayley Mills proposal to share senior moments?

50 Apple on many a desk
51 Supreme court count
52 Charity recipient
53 Old Testament book
57 Charro's rope
58 Dates for a BMOC
60 Kind of teaching
61 P. Diddy's first name
62 Johnny Tillotson ode on a painkiller?
67 Red Cross offering
68 It's bid by Burgundians
71 South Korean car company
72 Nobelist poet Sachs
74 Racket
75 Bobby Fuller Four saga of yardwork?
77 Protest attendee
86 It floods Florence
87 Oregon's capital
88 Dewlap
92 Sea of Tranquillity site
93 Nixon defense secretary Melvin

95 ZZ Top, e.g.
96 Melville title meaning "rover"
97 Johnny Nash confession of presbyopia?
102 Bristle-like part
104 Fur seal's cousin
105 Notwithstanding
106 "The Scourge of God"
108 Wasting away in Margaritaville?
109 Skip
112 The Beatles ballad on balding?
116 Miner matter
118 Certain titled retirees
123 "Curses!"
124 Sly & the Family Stone plug for an antidepressant?
127 Film director Clair
128 Four Holy Roman emperors
129 Collars
130 It merged with BP in 1998
131 Orbital organs
132 "The Little Colonel" of baseball

133 Gin liqueur flavorer
134 Baited

DOWN

1 Some hems come with them
2 Alternative to a lutz
3 Hitching goal
4 Arrived at in time
5 Remove, as loafers
6 Pola in silents
7 Tide type
8 Saharan
9 Ferret's cousin
10 Celebrant's vestment
11 Surrealist from Spain
12 Sedate
13 S-shaped molding
14 Swallow spots
15 Some plants like southern ones
16 Dependent or grandfather, e.g.
17 Rams, lambs, etc.
18 Kin of "The Swedish Nightingale"
24 E-mail address suffix
25 Most minute
30 Epsom event
32 John Hancock was one

34 "And giving ___, up the chimney ..."
36 Offhand, as a remark
37 San ___ (Ligurian Sea port)
38 Like leaning ltrs.
39 Break out
41 Indigent
42 "___ Pieces" (Peter & Gordon hit)
43 Doctrine
46 Formerly
47 Knee-slapper
48 Kind of gas
49 Prefix meaning half
54 Fervency
55 Fling reproaches (at)
56 Funny cohort of Morley, Lesley, etc.
59 Hindu sect member
63 Monet okay
64 Picker's target?
65 They go under tumblers
66 Compass dir.
68 Actor Arkin
69 The Flintstones' pet
70 Enthusiastic about
73 Finds fun
76 Carol refrain opening

77 Algerian port
78 Lesson segments
79 Evergreen shrub also known as furze
80 "Little Iodine" cartoonist
81 City near Oklahoma City
82 Princess in a 1977 hit movie
83 Virgilian "conqueror"
85 Starts
89 Upscale hotel chain
90 Yews use
91 Brat Packer Rob
94 Give a hand
98 Notorious Columbia drug cartel
99 Economist Janeway
100 Lemon-like fruits
101 Football pass
102 Floor of a flat
103 Natural gas constituent
106 Cold duck brand by Gallo
107 Fervency
110 One of Reagan's attorneys general
111 Eloise, for one
113 Room ender
114 Room starter
115 Sgt., cpl., and others
117 And others
119 Quirinal Palace site
120 Polo shirt label
121 Edible kind of shell
122 Windows desktop item
125 Computer attachment?
126 Alt. to Showtime

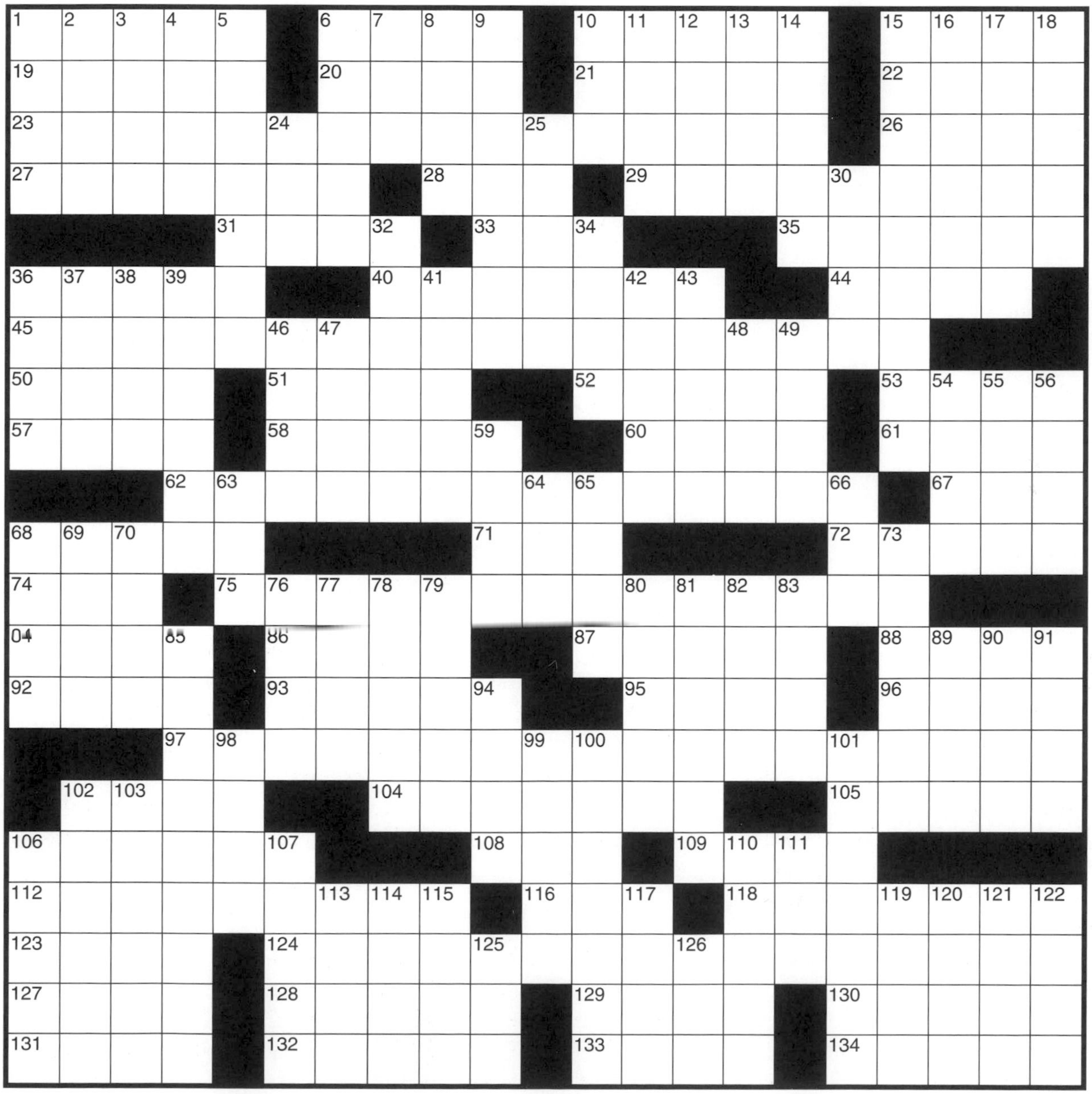

ANSWER, PAGE 92

31

WHERE THEY STAY

Places you've got to hear to believe

ACROSS

1 Witticism
5 Hall of Fame pitcher Rusie
9 Move like a cat
14 Its motto is "Industry"
15 He had many a two in tow
16 Samos and surrounds, once
17 Lodging for the kleptomaniac's convention?
20 Platter player
21 Still sealed
22 Wurst place
24 Brink
25 Pitching component
28 Went through the air?
30 Something that evokes "Go figure!"
35 Build-up remover brand
37 Seethe
39 Gnu girls
40 Lodging for the downsizing conference?
43 Aunt none of Princes Harry and William
44 Yak pack

45 It may leave one hanging
46 Vacation destination
48 Sophia Loren's birthplace
50 Catch
51 Satisfaction reactions
53 Battery part
55 Flood artificially
60 Cleans with elbow grease
64 Lodging for the self-improvement seminar?
66 Spin doctor's concern
67 Get worked up
68 Give up formally
69 Gave out sparingly
70 They may have a case
71 Legless lizard, for one

DOWN

1 Projects
2 Nice condition?
3 Rice-based drink
4 Show place?
5 Neighbor of Zaire and Zambia
6 Witticism
7 Most populous Hawaiian isle
8 Excel
9 "Peanuts" character
10 Kate Winslet's *Titanic* character
11 Getting ___ years
12 Bota content
13 Polaroid developer Edwin
18 Qui-Gon Jinn portrayer
19 Rice output
23 Site of many a pileup
25 Freud contemporary Felix
26 Seething
27 Famed clinic founders
29 Page, often
31 Prefix meaning one's own
32 Boarded
33 Attorney General before Thornburgh
34 Good point
36 Chihuahua child
38 Opposite of "in that case"
41 The Big Apple
42 Paris-based cousin of UNICEF
47 Tattered
49 Becomes engaged, in a way
52 Baby bird?
54 Role for Maria Callas
55 Bibliog. adverb
56 San ___, Italy
57 100 dinars
58 *Bus Stop* playwright
59 Sight from Presque Isle
61 Branch of an Austin coll.
62 Make over
63 Toy with runners
65 Tarzan portrayer Ron

ANSWER, PAGE 94

IN THE BALANCE

More suspense than comedy

ACROSS

1 Do squat
5 Staff at homes
10 Cloverleaf "leaf"
14 Austen title matchmaker
15 Anchor moving crane
16 Slanted, slightly?
17 Play tag, e.g.
19 One in a sub plot
20 Shredded
21 With 54-Across, emulates E.B. White's Charlotte?
23 Whole
26 Harmony section
27 Possess, after "thou"
30 Arizona Native American
32 Program file name suffix
33 Narnia's Aslan, e.g.
35 White's mouse
39 Relics of interest to archaeologists?
42 Flared apparel
43 "Oh, woe!"
44 "Oh, wow!"
45 Rootlessness
47 ATM input
48 Inedible kind of orange
51 Nader title _____
54 See 21-Across
56 Rock's _____ Dolls
60 Downey of *Touched By an Angel*
61 Lecherous, maybe?
64 Jack in many an oater
65 Tearful queen of Thebes
66 Its muscle relaxes in the dark
67 Root beer brand
68 Skin digs
69 Side by side?

DOWN

1 Riga resident
2 Typee capital
3 Sino-Russian river
4 Be realistic
5 Make fit
6 "At Seventeen" singer
7 VHS alternative
8 Mahler's *Symphony of a Thousand*, e.g.
9 Colonnade
10 Shirley Temple feature
11 Bikini event, briefly
12 Dance with Caribbean origins
13 Gambits
18 No Mr. Nice Guy, he
22 Service groups?
24 Pop singer Tori
25 Hold
27 Juno's counterpart
28 Lipinski leap
29 Weigh station sight
31 Jessica of *Dark Angel*
33 Property owner, often
34 Not _____ many words
36 With 57-Down, *Young Frankenstein* fraulein portrayer
37 Cant
38 Omegas
40 Pair such as pare/reap
41 Roars at some rings
46 Organic food item?
47 Illinois River city
48 Performed a scull operation
49 Robe of ancient *feminae*
50 Football star/sportscaster Rashad
52 See eye to eye
53 Bay City roller?
55 Fritzi, to Nancy
57 See 36-Down
58 Award started by N.Y.C.'s *Village Voice*
59 Greek peak
62 Dandy
63 Honour rec'd. by J.K. Rowling

ANSWER, PAGE 96

IN BLACK AND WHITE
They were albs, of course

ACROSS

1 Ballroom dance
6 Travesty
13 Old rope fiber
18 Kilts pattern
19 Downtowner, in baseball lingo
20 One of Donald's exes
21 Start of a verse
24 Hat, figuratively
25 Musical Shaw and Melvin
26 Make bubbly
27 Atom-like
29 Satirist Tom and anchor Jim
32 Darlin'
35 Lunch order
38 Seeks redress
39 Recall?
43 Alamogordo event
45 Rabble
47 List
49 Donnybrook
50 Line 2 of the verse
55 Hawaiian coffee
56 Sea below Italy's boot
57 Marx Brothers film setting
58 Achilles ___
60 Two-year-old, often
64 Menotti opera lad
67 With 41-Down, a famous Red Wing
69 Standard
73 Line 3 of the verse
78 Mill shipment
79 Keen on

80 Make sure (for oneself)
81 Serve, as mulligatawny
82 In ___ (agreeing)
01 Amnesia Lippo getup
86 Urban woe
89 Pink Floyd cofounder Barrett
90 Making up (for)
93 Christmastime
95 Composer born near Warsaw
98 ER subject
101 Shawm descendant
105 End of the verse
109 "Goodnight ___"
110 Faithful
111 Looked up and down?
112 Traffic markers
113 Visual offense
114 George at Gettysburg

DOWN

1 Haggle
2 Chow chow chow
3 Deal with brutally
4 German composer
5 Timber trimmer
6 Brigadoon producer Crawford
7 Novelist Victoria
8 Not your, in Tours
9 Delight (in)
10 Stems
11 Grayish brown
12 Like the BBC: Abbr.
13 Edmonton hockey player
14 Loath
15 Asia's ___ Kum desert
16 Troop group
17 Knight club
22 Grammy winner Cantrell

23 Calpurnia's husband
28 Analogy phrase
30 Outer covering
31 Mariner's danger
32 Sell on the street
33 Galba's successor
34 Brightly colored
36 Part of PABA
37 La Traviata tenor, in film
40 Swamp peril, briefly
41 See 67-Across
42 Possesses
44 Wrap snugly
46 It has many packs: Abbr.
48 Galba's predecessor
51 Ladders to Fire author
52 Coal porter
53 Main menu options
54 C.S. Lewis fictional realm

59 K-12
61 Car flop of '57
62 Carnival site
63 Judge in stripes
64 Book after Joel
65 Next-to-last of the Tudors
66 Yemeni port
68 Like "23 skiddoo" and "erst": Abbr.
70 Pari-mutuel concern
71 Count (on)
72 TV neigher and sayer
74 Chant
75 Jolt
76 French "roast"
77 "What ___ is new?"
83 1930s Atlanta inmate
85 Erroneous
87 Awaiting creating
88 Sound from a dungeon
91 Poops
92 "Yuck!"
94 Skier's accommodations
95 Modish
96 Successful lifeguard
97 Playwright Davis
99 Concerning
100 Operator
102 Gaucho's weapon
103 Had bills
104 The Night of the Iguana author
106 Packed in sardines
107 Turn on the sprinklers
108 ___ Perignon

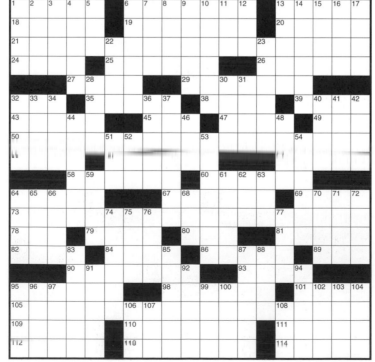

ANSWER, PAGE 82

VEGETARIAN'S NIGHTMARE

Anyone feel like roasting *Cathy*?

ACROSS

1 Pound down
5 Father of Zeus
11 Frilly neckpiece
16 Morales in movies
17 Big cheese
18 Blow away, in a way
19 Specialty butcher?
22 First Super Bowl winners
23 Sculpting medium
24 ___-Caps (kind of candy)
25 Weekly wds.
26 It may make a basket
29 Bearing
30 Butcher's lucrative offering?
34 Weight
35 Their bread's available at 3 A.M.
36 Messed up
40 Pound sound
41 Yes or no follower
43 Popular pasta
45 Butcher's boast?
48 Emulates Charon

49 Charon's destiny
50 Way to go
51 John who married a Duke
52 Two-year-old's assertion
53 Joke ending
54 Meeting at the butcher's?
59 Meaty reading
62 Long-stemmed?
63 Green standard
64 "Gotcha!"
65 Human's tail?
66 Will matters
70 Putting some soles on meat at the butcher's?
75 Like an abstract
76 Highly ornamental style
77 Wild party
78 A long time

79 Correctly
80 Basset asset

DOWN

1 Sub of a sort
2 Out of port
3 Painter Chagall
4 Acts disinterested in, as food
5 Elvis oater of 1969
6 Baseball's Swoboda and Guidry
7 Ottawa's prov.
8 Sgt., for one
9 Wave band abbr.
10 Historical council
11 Ronald's ex
12 "What ___, chopped liver?"

13 Opera buffi, usually
14 Layer on high
15 Mortise partner
20 It's on hand
21 Shade shade
26 Seldom opposite
27 "-ish," in age approximations
28 Return letters
29 Raise basis
30 Borders
31 Elbow grease
32 Hack riders
33 Mole, in dermatology
34 Israeli port
37 Take turns
38 Runaway bride
39 Where hash is "sweep the kitchen"
41 Back on a shelf

42 Montréal, for one
43 Event at state fairs
44 Spirit of St. Louis?
46 Crows, e.g.
47 Old TV's "___ Derringer"
52 Writer Wolitzer
53 Attach, as a backpack
55 Early New York Met Chacon
56 It's felt on one's head
57 Result
58 Hoopster Archibald
59 Renoir's *Woman With a Cat* cat, e.g.
60 Heavy-traffic hub
61 Newswoman Shriver
65 Rubs out
66 Delineate
67 Banderillero's target
68 1 joule – 10,000,000 ___
69 Terrier type
71 Musket butt?
72 Rocky pinnacle
73 It's here at the Louvre
74 Yule quaff

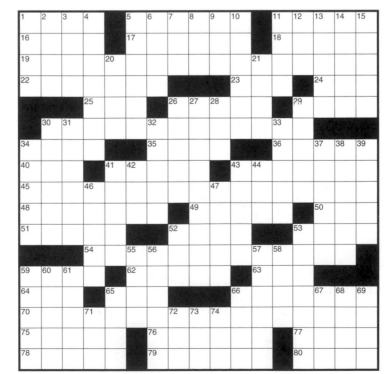

ANSWER, PAGE 84

SAME DIFFERENCE
A poser for the logophiles

ACROSS
1 Get a new loan on, briefly
5 Past the curfew
9 Lower, in Havana
13 Lena in *Havana*
14 Havana, for one
15 All-nighter follower, often
16 Start of a riddle
18 A meaning of -y
19 Put in position
20 Happily engages
22 A Turner
23 They support people
25 Part 2 of the riddle
32 Some Spanish?
33 Eeyore's loss
34 Helmet part
35 Trawl
36 Where to find the riddle's answer

38 Procter and Gamble detergent
39 *Missa* segment
41 A Turner
42 Blow gently
43 Part 3 of the riddle
46 Nettle
47 Yes man?
48 Rose type
51 Mainstays
55 Pardon seeker's lead-in
56 End of the riddle
59 Broccoli spearer
60 Words like "crossword," e.g.

61 Volcano peak
62 Slayer of Typhoeus
63 Subject of modern engineering
64 Often-patched spot

DOWN
1 Rank and file
2 For all grades, briefly
3 Decree
4 Knows unconsciously
5 Long sentence?
6 Past
7 ___ cross
8 Page task
9 *Animal House* star

10 Cartesian coordinates reference
11 Boxer La Motta
12 "My Cup Runneth Over" singer Ed
14 Spoil, perhaps
17 Drink from fermented rice
21 Whimpers
23 Mint process
24 Francis of *The Thrill of It All*
25 Hero, maybe
26 Winter *mes*
27 Tribal emblem
28 English poet laureate, 1785–90
29 Laker in *Kazaam* and *Steel*

30 Lord's laborers
31 A sister of Thalia
36 Egyptian Christians
37 Trail mix ingredients
40 Prescription information
42 Paul Lynde was one on *Bewitched*
44 Camp activity
45 Sandy sediment
48 Airhead
49 Old comics character Kabbible
50 Windows feature
51 Window's feature
52 Shortly
53 Sandberg at second
54 *Peter Pan* pirate
57 Kind of dancing
58 Back burner?

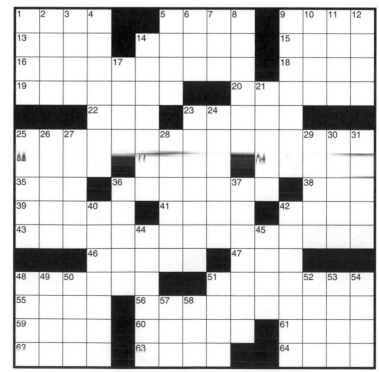

ANSWER, PAGE 86

STRESS REDUCTION
What a difference a syllable makes

ACROSS
1 Children's author Lowry
5 Pac-10 sch.
9 Talk show host Jack
13 Opera and film basso Tajo
15 Where to watch the gnus
16 Memo Latin
17 With 25-Across, quote from *Macbeth* about a candle?
20 Old coin of Europe
21 He's best known for *Kojak*
22 Bass, e.g.
24 Stands
25 See 17-Across
30 Head start?
31 "Narnia" lion
32 Score less eight

36 ___ onto (grab)
38 Popeye creator Elzie
40 Four-legged father
41 Meaning of "Fitz-"
43 Stately
45 Put the kibosh on
46 Sneeze, often?
49 On the briny
51 Coolidge, the singer
52 Edgar or Hugo winners
54 Patron of doctors and artists
58 Cheese crocks, wine casks, etc?
61 God of love
62 Museum pieces

63 Perturbed
64 Men's planet?
65 Pentagon problem
66 Tries ryes

DOWN
1 Thing, a thing!
2 Nebraska native or country
3 Pet food brand
4 Gets a piece of Z action?
5 Israeli submachine gun
6 One in a pen
7 Birlers' supports
8 Teeming
9 *Guernica* et al.

10 Bracelet site
11 Environs
12 Rose, Bench, etc.
14 Canada's capital
18 Torment
19 Like many a campus building
23 First Ladies Julia and Letitia
25 License plates
26 Seat of Hawaii County
27 Ocher component
28 Goals on ice
29 Ancient catapult
33 WWW publication

34 O'Brien-Moore of *Peyton Place*
35 Deli worker's cry
37 Mafiosi
39 Relish vegetable
42 Makes tracks
44 Alphanumeric unit
47 Scolding
48 Swiss canton
49 Bakery product
50 Sea in the Indian Ocean
52 "Bang!"
53 Achy
55 Citric hybrid
56 Castle stronghold
57 Actor Byrnes and baseballer Roush
59 "Player" in protein synthesis
60 Sound of scorn

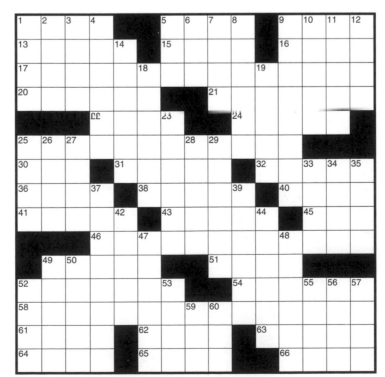

ANSWER, PAGE 88

37

U S OF A

With US-A trade in the spotlight

ACROSS

1 Katmandu's country
6 Polish applications
11 Omar's *Doctor Zhivago* role
15 Rock singer Ocasek
18 Flabbergast
19 Nape
20 Zoomed
21 NYC home of *The Starry Night*
22 What the crazy sculptor had?
25 Recedes
26 Oktoberfest souvenir
27 Account
28 Works with dough
30 Trig ratio
32 "Goodbye for now, Mr. Sheen"?
34 Layette item
37 Filmdom's Franco, pianist Peter, etc.
39 Exiguous
40 Bas-relief material
41 Activated
43 Argentina's Buenos ___
45 Took in or let down
47 Puzzling singer?
50 Breaks forth
54 Saw things
55 Tog (up)
56 He may have a crush on you
58 Cameo
59 Airport limo alternative
61 The Gaels' school
62 Keen sounds
64 Rose type
65 Disgruntled 2000 election remark?
69 *Politically Incorrect*'s Iditarod man?
71 Spanish diminutive
72 Driving hazard
73 Wurst case place
74 Small belt?
75 "Phooey!"
77 Unexacting
78 Sea bordering Kazakhstan
79 Dance to "Hernando's Hideaway"
83 Make a bundle, maybe
85 Tin Man's financial problem?
89 Sound of hail
92 Nerve gas in 1995 Tokyo news
93 *The Lion King* baddie
94 They're stacked in contests
97 Actresses Loughlin and Singer
99 Marathoner's units
101 Woolly lassie
102 Antithesis of bedtime prayers?
105 Winged
107 Subordinate
108 Bluish-greens
110 Close friend of Debussy
113 Currency exchange fee
114 Beefeater's song on a windy day?
118 Ala. neighbor
119 Conservative in history
120 Singer/bandleader Skinnay
121 Find irresistible
122 Saving places, for short
123 Further
124 Do a double take, e.g.
125 Joint partner?

DOWN

1 Collar
2 Pests, to many Aussie farmers
3 Over
4 Tezcucan ancient
5 An MRI may find one
6 It airs TV's *Crossfire*
7 Beat on tests
8 *Sieben* follower
9 God, Greek-style
10 Buffalo hockey team
11 Designer monogram
12 Candid
13 Direct to a detour
14 Pastoral poem
15 Rosie of *The Jetsons* and others
16 Steeps
17 Palance played him in *Che!*
21 Botched
23 Shorts line
24 Ophthalmologist's offering
29 German pistol
31 Stoltz of *Chicago Hope*
33 Nathan Hale's alma mater
34 Ward who played Robin in *Batman*
35 "Amazing Grace" ending
36 Nancy newborn
38 Emit
42 From Friesland
44 Made smart
46 Spheres
48 Big Persian cats?
49 Mrs. McKinley
51 Course
52 Organizational diagram, often
53 Texas flag symbol
56 Island east of Java
57 Sea otter endangerer
60 Modern kind of train

61 Alpine goat
62 Tale Tell?
63 Bridge groups ...
65 ... and declarations
66 The Osmonds' home
67 Resentful
68 ___ culpa
69 Wampum

70 Quarrels
73 Dr. with *The Chronic* album
76 Layered pastry
78 Left Bank dweller, maybe
80 Cote d'Azur resort
81 Erode
82 Shrek, e.g.
84 Shade source

85 Saturn and Mercury, e.g.
86 Mesozoic period
87 Brooklet
88 Apprehensive
90 Plastering material?
91 Sauternes servers
94 Codeine is one

95 Quasimodo's job
96 Sprites
98 Woody Guthrie collaborator
100 ___ *Mater* (Latin hymn)
103 Sergei, Russia's first premier
104 Rhone feeder

106 Chopin piece
109 Girl in *Light in August*
111 "The race ___!"
112 Zaragoza's river
115 Reuben base
116 Abbr. on Rockies schedules
117 Itch

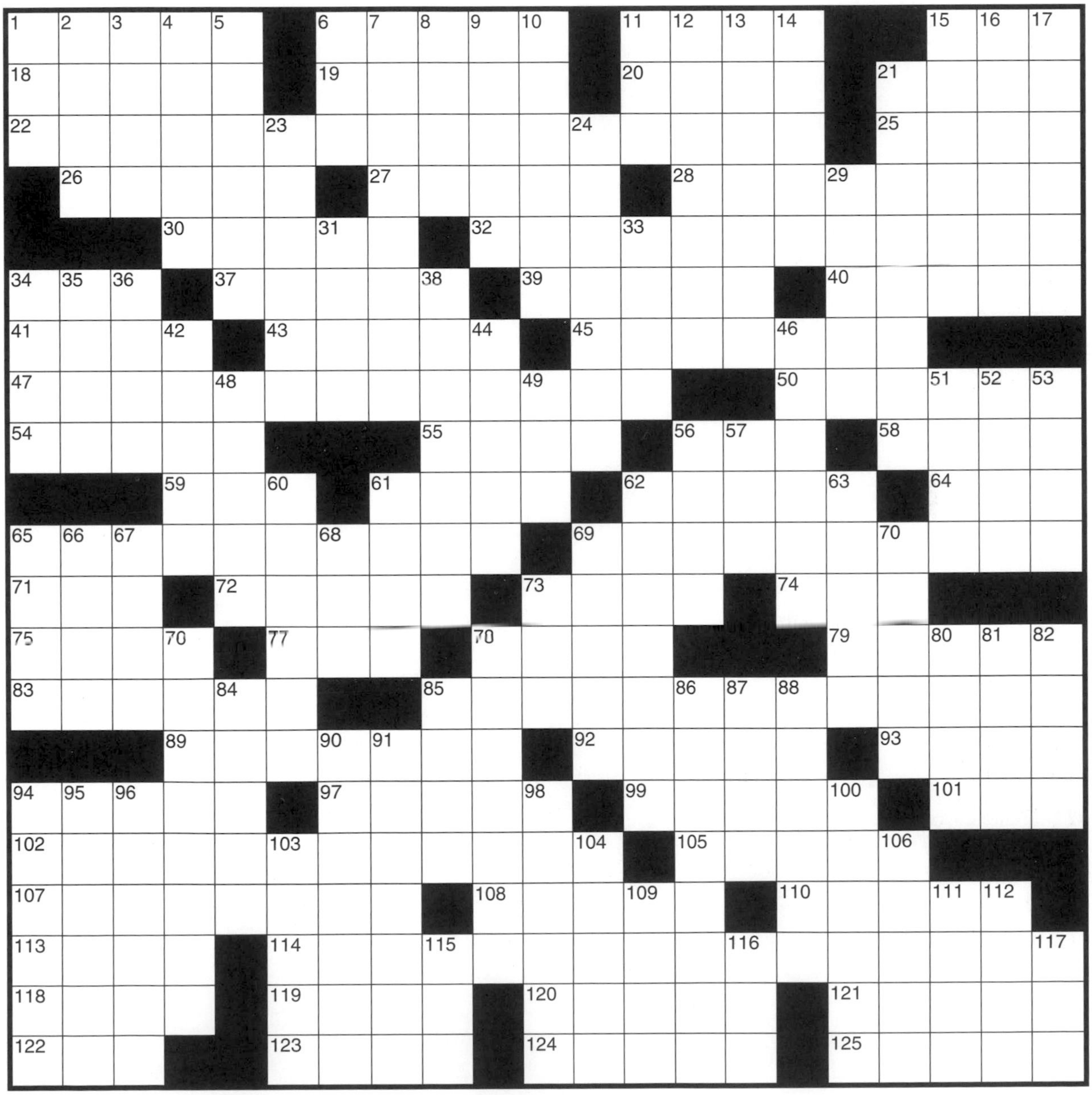

APT APPELLATIONS
Women in action

ACROSS

1 Kind of veto
7 Vivid display
12 Guitarist's gadget
16 Wrinkle remover
17 Swollen enough to knead
18 Port west of Algiers
19 SHE'S PRONE TO A SPORTS INJURY?
21 Like some breakfast cereals
22 Bulgar, for example
23 Eye part
24 Round receptacle
26 Support site pro
29 Part of APB: Abbr.
30 Become prone
31 ___-Magnon man
33 SHE'S A CEO?
37 Tag sale stuff
39 Messy kid's "handkerchief"
40 Julia's *Seinfeld* role
41 Luke, to Darth Vader
42 "Chair person" Charles
46 Layettes, trousseaux, etc.
47 SHE DEALS WITH WHEELS?
51 Round chocolate-caramel candy
52 Hungarian's neighbor, perhaps
54 Groza of gridiron fame
55 Corkscrew, e.g.
57 Sportscaster known for his mouth
59 Typical
60 SHE'S A DISHONEST CLERK?
64 Fleur-de-___
65 Fond du ___, Wisconsin
66 Lodge dweller's construction
67 Speakers' platforms
69 First name in speed-reading
71 Leo, for one
73 Old Testament book
76 Henley happening
77 SHE'S A MODEL?
81 Flying biter
82 Trim
83 Spring
84 Slangy mouths
85 Explorer Meriwether
86 Organizational scheme

DOWN

1 Drupe-center group
2 Intravenous alternative
3 SHE'S A COOK?
4 Rascal
5 Snaky swimmer
6 Athlete's head?
7 Stuck out courageously
8 Rickey ingredient
9 On the QE2
10 Buddhist movement
11 Express eagerness, colloquially
12 Rail family bird
13 Fit to be farmed
14 Specialized lingo
15 Agate varieties
20 Baedeker book
25 Bustling
27 Warner Oland film character
28 Idealist German philosopher
29 Good, in Guadalajara
31 Musical buildup, briefly
32 Potentate
34 Rifle type
35 Common interest group
36 Start of a well-known hymn
38 Behave wrongly, old-style
43 SHE'S A KEENING WOMAN?
44 Mournful poem
45 Band-Aid targets
48 Small intestine part
49 Colloidal dispersions
50 Rambles
53 Sycophant
56 Like Eloise of fiction
58 Tabloid topic
59 Surrounded by
60 White collar workers?
61 Cuban cigar
62 Polar covering
63 Generous donations
68 Branch, to Brutus
70 Court do-overs
71 Wet blanket?
72 Crucifix inscription
74 In bygone days
75 Goblet part
78 Keats feat
79 They're firmed by crunches
80 Trigger's rider

ANSWER, PAGE 92

CASEWORK
Not for detectives only

ACROSS
1 *Scarface* group
6 Genesis son
10 Cooler
14 Twisty-horned mammal
15 Certain Pueblo
16 Ferrari in car history
17 SHOWCASE?
20 Apollo spacecraft part
21 Rex's stout tec
22 Face down?
23 Pencil holder, perhaps
24 Sand castle mold
26 SUITCASE?
34 Six Flags feature
35 Television producer Michaels
36 "Botch-___" (Rosemary Clooney song)
37 *Ars Amatoria* author
38 Spin preceder
39 Spill the beans
40 Society page French
41 Married lady of song
42 Idaho's Coeur d'___
43 CRANKCASE?
46 Actor Mischa
47 Part of WPM
48 It's a nut case
51 Teen's trailer?
53 Knot-tying phrase
56 BRIEFCASE?
60 Polaris bear
61 Comb makers
62 *The Threepenny Opera* composer
63 The third man
64 Obi, for one
65 Edge horizontally

DOWN
1 Complain
2 Skin lotion additive
3 It may be full of pens
4 It may fill pens
5 Shelley elegy
6 Ivan the Terrible, e.g.
7 Self, for a start
8 BYOB mailing
9 Nonexistent
10 Many faceted things
11 Historical novelist Seton
12 Atom ender
13 Lady's man?
18 Polypody plant
19 Tolerate
23 Scanned
24 3.26 light years
25 *Comus* composer
26 Tine
27 Dietary iron source
28 Versailles goodbye
29 Engineless aircraft
30 Geometric kind of section
31 Agricultural machine
32 Saudi neighbor
33 Ancient Mediterranean ship
38 Comedian Martha
39 Sub alternatives
41 Mettle
42 *The Sound of Music* star
44 Paper products company
45 Washstand topper
48 Greenish-blue
49 Restrain
50 Chantilly's department
51 Pros
52 Effuse
53 Footnote abbr.
54 Mentally slow
55 Make like a rake
57 Charcoal bag abbr.
58 Verily
59 *Agnus ___*

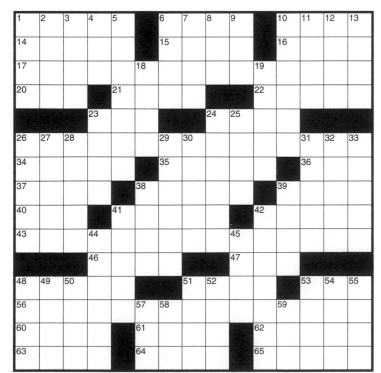

ANSWER, PAGE 94

THE SCOOP
A hand-packed selection of dippy puns

ACROSS

1 Sheltie shelter provider
5 Refuse
10 Plácido's homeland
16 Monopoly gamepiece
17 Some porters
19 Wastes not
20 Kind of suit
21 Sucker flavor?
23 Inner: Prefix
24 Charlotte of *Bananas*
25 Get off (from)
26 Investment
27 Good one
29 Pathetic
31 Turner of Hollywood
33 Sydney's state: Abbr.
34 Language kin of Hopi
35 Flavor that has punch?
39 Bug
41 Gotten high
42 Furry *Star Wars* creature
46 Giving mommy lip, e.g.
47 "... two fives for ___?"
48 See 69-Across
50 With the bow, in music
52 Rip-off flavor?
56 Hoopster Shaq
57 France's Cote-___
58 A peer
59 Oil of ___
61 Harare-to-Nairobi dir.
62 Kind of acid
64 Good ol' boy's flavor?

68 Vaudeville performers
69 With 48-Across, an award-winning flavor?
71 Mod designer Gernreich
72 Nagpur nanny
74 Some gobblers
75 Craving
78 Anxiety
81 Golf club flavor?
84 Unspecified
85 CEO's deg.
88 Needing kneading, maybe
89 Salt
90 Waffle cone feature
92 Lingo
94 Film director Petri
97 Paris's ___ de Rivoli
99 Lowdown
100 Flavor that only comes in cups?

103 Winning feeling
104 Pi and such
105 Tenants
106 Jack of *Big Bad John*
107 Center of ancient Macedonia
108 Brands
109 "Phooey!"

DOWN

1 Appraises
2 Turn palm-down
3 Lousy flavor?
4 Composer Bruckner
5 Daddy Warbucks's assistant
6 Abrogate
7 *Shell and Head* sculptor
8 What shaken soft drink bottles do
9 Fictional tea party host
10 Directional suffix
11 Attacks

12 When repeated, an engine sound
13 Thai, for one
14 Hourglass parts
15 Out of kilter
17 It starts in Mar.
18 Cone sizes
22 Pointless
28 Some Feds
30 ___ by Chocolate (rich dessert)
32 Now, to Nero
36 Coffee has one
37 Domain
38 Ell, as in Monticello
40 Additionally
42 Velvet finish
43 One of those soft-serve "twist" flavors?
44 Praying figure
45 Scottish straits
47 Censorship fighter: Abbr.
49 Cry used in driving animals

50 Take on
51 The rich kid in *Nancy*
53 Sphere
54 Hanna-Barbera bear
55 Sing opposite
58 Old French coin
60 Certain stove
63 Mensa measures
65 Spreadable cheese
66 Veep before Clinton
67 Skilled
68 Bern's river
70 Know biz?
73 Darn
76 Old number?
77 Pen-shaped
79 Beg
80 Kind of analysis
81 Tear-jerking quality
82 Person on the payroll
83 Las ___, NM
85 1984 Men's Slalom gold medalist
86 Moolah
87 Burnishing tool
91 Trimming tool
93 Groucho's role in *A Night at the Opera*
95 Finishes a Baskin-Robbins item
96 River in D-Day news
98 Common Canadian interjections
101 "Prepared" grp.
102 Hagen of Broadway

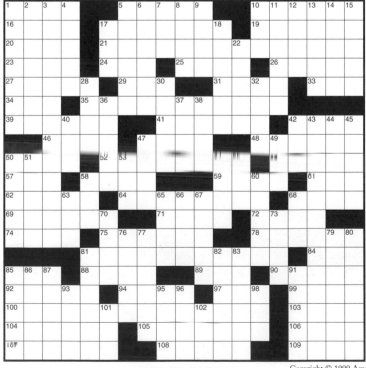

ANSWER, PAGE 96

CAMPING TRIP

Try not to stumble

ACROSS

1 Horse race ratio
5 Fast horse
9 Kind of key
15 Spelling in acting
16 X'd from text
18 Wool source
19 Divorcee's unlikely ode?
21 Christie sleuth
22 Lawn product brand
23 Where jailbirds feed?
25 Sail holder
27 Mandolin's cousin
28 Sculpted form
31 Roasting rod
33 Lady of the knight
37 Singing talents?
40 Pickling spice
41 Start to knock?
42 Oscar Mayer rival
43 Flame-thrower substance
44 Arrest
45 Hide from a Kettle?
47 Snicker's half
48 Jibes
50 *Cheers* support
51 Arthur and Benaderet on TV

52 They're supported by cheers
53 In re a relative's cold symptom?
55 Mr. Rubik
56 "Slammin' Sammy"
57 Hub near the Loop
58 Piquancy
60 Mozart's age when he wrote his Fifth
62 Back-stabbing office-holder?
67 Papiamento's spoken there
72 Recipe quantity, often
73 Do it to get this puzzle's theme
75 Ballot snafu follow-up

76 Play the ukulele
77 For two, in scores
78 Made a basket?
79 Just fair
80 Peru's patron *santa*

DOWN

1 One of F.A.O. Schwarz's names
2 Saloon swinger
3 "Shucks!"
4 Nonverbal "Shucks!"
5 Arc suffix
6 Gaucho's rope
7 Service center?
8 "The ___" (telly company)
9 Plan in detail
10 Soaring
11 Added pizazz to

12 Edible starchy tuber
13 Alan Greenspan concern: Abbr.
14 Deserters
17 XC × VI
20 *Lou Grant* reporter Joe
24 Whiffenpoof Society members
26 Bohemian dances
28 Scarlet ___ (songbird)
29 Muffin material
30 Yastrzemski stat
31 "My Way" crooner
32 Basil-based sauces
34 Newbie
35 Travel allowance

36 Tangle up
37 Woolly
38 Part finisher
39 Graduate student papers
40 Tram, e.g.
43 Willie of country fame
45 Caesar's foot
46 ___ polloi
49 Face made with punctuation
51 Plumy neckpiece
53 Comic strip possum
54 Fraud
56 Shot from the shadows
59 Sharp
60 Part of TNT
61 Anatomical anvil
62 "Beetle Bailey" creator Walker
63 From the top
64 Stubbs of the Four Tops
65 High points
66 Tendo tots
68 Raise
69 Reverse
70 A/C measures
71 On liners, maybe
74 Medical provider grp.

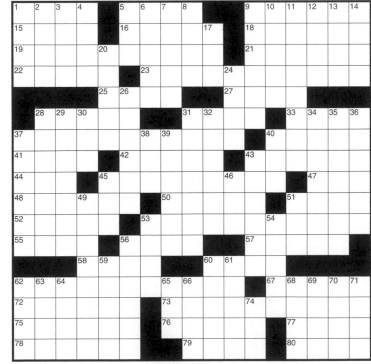

ANSWER, PAGE 81

GOING POSTAL

Some "mixed company" wordplay

ACROSS

1 Bridge doings
6 They're spent in Vientiane
10 Pest control brand
14 Sets on
15 Nonflammable spark
16 Bring down
17 Minute Maid Park player
18 Leopold's partner-in-crime
19 That one: Latin
20 Start of a "B.C." query
23 Snake-like swimmers
24 Smudge cause
27 Priest's vestments
30 Bonanza
32 Played a siren
33 Forget it, in Fife
34 Soybean product
35 With dispatch
36 Doc bloc
37 Part 2 of the query

40 Comics' Flapp and Fuzz: Abbr.
41 Frequent Mastroianni costar
43 Chic
44 LAPD initial
45 Thomas Gray was one
46 "___ beans!" ("Excellent!")
47 Vega's constellation
48 Well brought-up
50 Bring down, British-style
52 End of the query
57 Slangy knife
59 Titans' mother, in myth

60 Herber or Weinmeister of football fame
61 Actress Skye
62 Each and all, poetically
63 Punning part of the query's answer
64 Arthur Rubinstein's Polish birthplace
65 Pullman boycott leader
66 Four-time Pulitzer poet

DOWN

1 *Pygmalion* playwright
2 Rebuke

3 Nick Charles's dog
4 Tuesday in Toledo
5 Vermont ski resort
6 Eliminates
7 Teraph
8 Shrimp
9 Fencer's pick
10 Withers
11 Way one may be deprived
12 Jed Clampett's find
13 Salem-to-Portland dir.
21 Think ___ (judge unfavorably)
22 Andromeda, e.g.
25 Manse dweller

26 Macedonian city
27 Like clocks with hands
28 "The style," on dessert menus
29 Remember
31 Caused by
34 Hair stylist role
38 Jamb containers
39 China's Zhou ___
42 Costar of *The Breakfast Club*
46 Split
47 "Masochism Tango" creator Tom
49 Followed up on booing, maybe
51 Symbol of authority
53 Certain Slav
54 Bring down
55 One of a dozen popes
56 Nat'l Literacy mo.
57 Part of RSVP
58 Half of a chocolate drink name

ANSWER, PAGE 83

DIG IT

Let's hear a "Bonanza!" when you're done

ACROSS

1 Animal protection org.
5 Some Beemer's beams
9 401(k), e.g.
13 Fairy tale penultimate
14 Polyphonic choral piece
15 Stir (up)
16 Takes a break at the gold dig?
19 Frees, maybe
20 Lure
21 Its rides aren't round-trip
23 Potted kind of pet
24 Gold digger's cry?
30 Caen's river
31 Name on denim pockets
32 Tilted, British-style
33 Like an ENT's deg.
34 Restaurant diner's concern
37 Cpl., e.g.
38 Mother of Ashley and Wynonna

40 It's not pleasant to evoke
41 Small dishful
42 What they said about the gold digger's work?
16 Stromboli's "cousin" in Sicily
47 Hockey player Mikita
48 Gloves, parka, goggles, etc.
51 Needing ironing?
55 Gold digging for fun, not profit?
58 Admits
59 Less explicable
60 X is one

61 Nuts and bolts
62 Cage, for a Blackhawk
63 It's trapped in the dryer

DOWN

1 Land of Lake Titicaca
2 Level
3 Kind of run
4 Monet, e.g, in Evian
5 Pardo or Ho
6 "Who am ___ say?"
7 He's a pain
8 Scope start
9 Assess in calculated shares
10 Something in a Bursa purse

11 One who played Obi-Wan
12 Digs for chicks
14 Metz's river
17 Ward on TV
18 Archie's imperative to Edith
22 No loafer, this one
24 Eminent
25 Bless, in a way
26 Dickens
27 Mot Cot pagoda site
28 Ancient Machu Picchu resident
29 Word with whistle or door
30 Erstwhile Atlanta venue

34 Mary-Kate, to Ashley
35 Dench/Winslet title role of 2001
36 Mythical horse-man
39 "She" may be a lifesaver
41 Neighbor of Mali
43 Computer type
44 Texas town of song
45 Windmill part
48 Tinseltown problem
49 Fruit also known as Chinese gooseberry
50 Quarters en route
52 More than calf-length
53 Common ER cry
54 "___ Moi" (*Camelot* song)
56 Abbr. on toothpaste tubes
57 Toothpaste choice

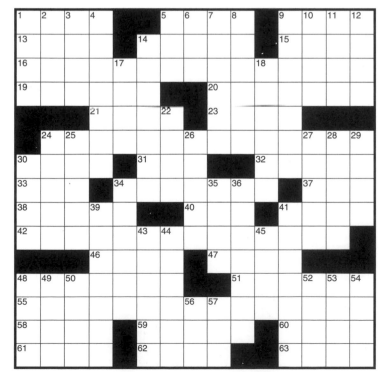

LAUGHTEREFFECTS

A little cruciverb-L-ism

ACROSS

1 Vichy "very"
5 Abbr. on a business sign
10 Carnival entry
14 Modern speed measure
18 Witness oath antepenultimate
19 Biological hollow
20 Pub missile
21 Heche of *Wag the Dog*
22 Good citizen's lament?
24 What the heel behaved like?
26 Singer O'Connor who had no-hair days
27 Highest, on diplomas
29 Fallow
30 Hi-tech diagnostic tool
31 "___ bleu!"
32 Nest
33 Eight bells, perhaps
05 Follow a cannibal's cookbook step?
40 Piece of a bun
41 Concerns of Alfred Binet: Abbr.
44 Kind of drag
45 Pound sound
46 *National Velvet* horse name

47 Briard's brood
49 Some are pinked
51 Look villainous?
57 *Encounter in April* poet May
59 O.T. book
61 Disney's middle name
62 Zombie ingredient
63 Deck
64 Museum shop buys
67 Small soldier?
68 Fragrance by Dana
69 Result of spilling sunscreen on a fan?
73 Punjab monotheist
75 Fact finisher
76 Assertions
77 Give off
80 Plumb of *The Brady Bunch*
81 Famed painter of Giverny
83 Okla. neighbor
84 Brought up
85 With 121-Across, Regis's words to a cavalry general?
88 Bath water quantity
91 Precious prefix

92 ___ *Poetica* (Horace treatise)
93 Marsh
95 Its head gets in last
96 Lush
97 Durations
100 What the twins used for sleeping in the den?
105 Certain cat
107 Ophidian fish
108 Authors Vicki and L. Frank
111 Simpson trial judge
112 Where it's always peak season
113 Corsairs' vessel of yore
116 Its effects were weathered
118 What to say to a boor?
121 See 85-Across
123 Lotto-like gambling game
174 One in a martial relationship
125 Does something with files or flies
126 Drops flies, e.g.
127 Mlle., in Mallorca
128 Period often put in letters?

129 They cried in *On Golden Pond*
130 Numskull

DOWN

1 Demonstrative pronoun
2 Some mortgage deals, briefly
3 Pairs skater Leonova
4 Address
5 Memorable stretch
6 Makes shirring
7 Vegan's staple
8 "Class of" class
9 In a soothing way
10 It watches what you eat
11 Sculler's task
12 Mass sections
13 Met basso Tajo
14 Amt. still owed
15 Lack of social norms
16 Follows up on frisking
17 Goes against
19 Shire chiefs of yore
23 Julie's *Doctor Zhivago* role
25 Soup veggies
28 Wing it
34 Corner
36 Dagwood, to Cookie

37 Tom Hanks film of 1988
38 Not like Stevie, this kind of wonder
39 Olympics event
41 Res ___ loquitor (the thing speaks for itself, in legal-speak)
42 It's often surrounded by dorms
43 Chain drive wheel
46 Paten
48 Erstwhile brewing company
50 Part of SST
52 It's set for rising
53 Actors' concerns
54 Evidence of errors
55 Drawback
56 Mustangs' sch.
58 Famed Dakota denizen
60 Roman woman's robe
64 "The Elder" Roman scholar
65 Isuzu model
66 Gridlock or locks problem
68 Astros' turf
70 Despoils

71 Undies style
72 Last word?
73 ___ whale (rorqual)
74 Hosp. drips
78 Game download freebie
79 Copy and paste, e.g.
81 Array, as for battle
82 One of the big brass
84 Marks down, maybe
86 Drape
87 Big name in watches
89 Bad stuff in cigarettes
90 Umbrella part
94 Merry
97 Results of some spills
98 Commotion
99 Administer a sickbed sacrament
100 Pair of opposite electrical charges
101 Actress Andress
102 White mouse, for one
103 Opening night event
104 Risked getting burned
106 Relieve
109 Start of something little?
110 One of Bergen's puppets
114 Car man Ferrari
115 Biblical killer
117 About
119 Hawaii's Mauna ___
120 Son of Odin
122 Hi-fi set?

WHINE TASTING

A "sour grapes" send-up (send back the bottle!)

ACROSS

1 Lew of silents and comedy
5 Superior of "The Sad Sack"
10 USAF look-see
15 Douay Bible book
16 Assumed handle
17 Mescal button
18 IT HAS A BOUQUET OF CHEAP PERFUME
20 Red flags
21 A treat, any day
22 ITS BODY IS NONE TOO SUBTLE
24 Scots variant of "Irish"
26 Lamprey-like
27 Auntie, to Dad
28 TALK ABOUT A GAMY NOSE!
33 He'd "kid you not"
34 Elm City collegians
35 "Let's get out of here!"
39 Hrs. before lunch
40 Printed copy
42 Capacitance units
44 THE PALATE IS PASTY
48 Proscriptions
49 *Cabaret* director Bob
50 Pewter, mostly
51 Indigo source

52 First-rate
53 Kind of yr.
54 THIS SURE HAS EARTHY UNDERPINNINGS
60 Welsh rabbit ingredient
63 Commotion
64 Platter on Far East menus
65 TASTES LIKE AN ANTACID
68 Workers in *R.U.R.*
72 Bassett who played Tina Turner
73 IT FINISHES FLAT
76 Mounts
77 Bird's "penthouse"
78 Breakfast food brand

79 Throng
80 Spray type
81 Smoothing tool

DOWN

1 Slews
2 Jacob's twin
3 Shaped by an ax
4 Certain cervid
5 Former state?
6 Eiger, e.g.
7 Grande opening?
8 Teri of *Young Frankenstein*
9 Values highly
10 Passes on
11 Ogler
12 Some pants, shortened
13 King of Germany, 936–973
14 Egg cups?

17 Painter Picasso
19 Almost unique
23 ___ *gratia* (Thanks be to God)
25 "If ___ Would Leave You" (*Camelot* song)
28 Oriental one-scull boat
29 Herb in Japanese dishes
30 Verve
31 Summon, at a hotel desk
32 Like unbleached linen
33 Orzo and such
36 Divination-related
37 Rather eccentric
38 Justin Timberlake's band

40 *Citizen Kane* film co.
41 Chicago loop group
42 Abbr. on monastery mail
43 Film rating number
45 SAT taker's goal
46 ___ fide
47 Deplete
52 Part of ANC
53 1997 Robin Williams comedy
55 Tristan's beloved
56 Lab burners of yore
57 Vita in a nutshell
58 Girl's name on cigars
59 Fairy tale second
60 Fluster
61 Presto opposite, in music
62 Gung-ho
66 Have to have
67 Mother of Hades
69 Gymnast Korbut
70 Sale items
71 Hit the mall
74 EMT destinations
75 Actress Vardalos of *My Big Fat Greek Wedding*

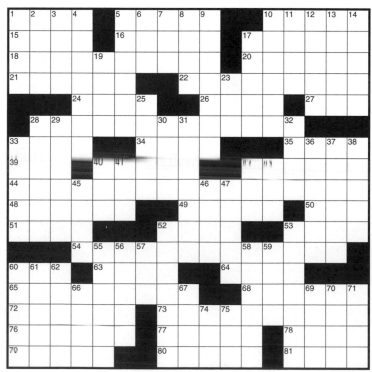

ANSWER, PAGE 89

THINK OUTSIDE THE BOX
There's no telling what you might accomplish

ACROSS

1 Finance pages acronym
5 Parsonage
10 Bursa
13 Like a human flock
14 Menotti title name
15 Times gone by
16 Chickmate?
17 Forbidden
19 Spinning
21 Dry, as wine
22 Part of a Punjab tab
23 Tightly packed tidbit
25 Russian "Mother of Cities"
27 Tree-to-be
28 Fictional septet member

31 It goes around laps in cars
35 More irritable
37 Book after Neh.
38 Grenadine is one
40 Put ___ act
41 Matador
43 Cantors, e.g.
45 Permanent sites
47 Airhead's lack
48 Part of MIT
49 Nacre sources
53 Home of the Orange Bowl
56 He might be Right: Abbr.
58 General Mills cereal
59 Like long meetings still in session

62 Mississippi feeder
63 Sean Connery, for one
64 Ward off
65 Punch server?
66 Oscar-winning composer ___ Dun
67 Meaning
68 Mavens

DOWN

1 Robert and Alan in films
2 Saint from Troyes
3 Duck down
4 Speeds
5 Long March leader
6 How grins are formed

7 ___ the Great (fictional boy detective)
8 Defibrillates
9 Mischief-maker
10 "Soul food" in book titles
11 *Rule, Britannia* composer
12 Surrender
15 "This is the last straw!"
18 Lineage
20 Dusseldorf "dear"
24 Actor Liam and kin
26 With klutziness
29 Web mag
30 It comes after the last slash
31 Fixed

32 Those señores
33 Trac II alternative
34 Start to dent?
36 TLC providers
39 Bares
42 1998 De Niro movie
44 Evict
46 Endeavored
50 Moral precept
51 Goal of some strikes
52 Openings
53 Necessity
54 Terrace-farming ancient
55 Author of many a quot.
57 Uniform
60 Beetle juice?
61 Way with no.'s

ANSWER, PAGE 91

PERSONAL COMPUTING
A human side of technology

ACROSS

1 1988 Quaid/Ryan thriller
4 Sandwich alternative
8 A pacer's position, figuratively
12 "Title" for Heidi Fleiss
17 Stethoscope part
19 Jazz singer Anita
20 Shampoo brand
21 Misplaced medicine container?
23 ___ Pradesh (Indian state)
24 Whined
25 Int'l. commerce group
26 Webhead?
28 Trompe l'___
29 Finsteraarhorn, for one
31 Midwife's announcement?
35 Head bone
39 Glassmaking mixture
40 Kind of bag
41 Popular ISP
42 Cheese, to some Swiss
44 Excitedly, musically
47 Result of too much exposure to *Barney*?
49 Fair weather feature
50 Bob Hoskins's role in *Hook*
51 Savings for sr.'s
52 Arabian gulf
53 Brillo competitor
54 Till over
57 Tense situations
59 Approves, initially
62 Ms. Brockovich

63 Nonclerical
64 Stave's neighbor
68 Brings aboard again
70 Mouths, at the breakfast table?
73 Metal-extracting substance
74 Pistol case
75 Actress Peeples
76 Mother of Zeus
77 Prefix with culture
78 IMAX movie mount
80 Get approval for a loan?
84 *Señor* ending
85 Bay
86 Poetic contraction
87 Film director Ang
89 ___ *Gay* (WWII B-29)
93 Burbs, boonies, etc.

95 Purpose of washing a kid's mouth with soap?
99 Vapid
100 Pump or pumpernickel part
101 Horse show event
102 One of the Von Trapp children
103 Spot
104 Of course
105 Article for Hugo

DOWN

1 *Chocolat* actor Johnny
2 Part of Honolulu County
3 Seed covering
4 Fauna
5 Cartoon chihuahua
6 Don't have this, man
7 Trivial
8 Half of a sob

9 Internet suffix for a college
10 Blood-sampling tool
11 ___ *Skip* (2000 film)
12 *The Sporting ___*
13 Robotize
14 See Ezio Pinza, e.g.?
15 Effective use
16 Haggard of country music
18 Song of praise
22 Much ado about nothing
27 Confounds
30 Feline "I feel fine"
32 Impels
33 Struggled
34 Like God, to some believers
35 Rotary parts
36 Share quarters
37 *"Der ___"* (Adenauer)

38 Get going, British-style
43 Dolt
44 Surrender
45 WBA stat
46 Kvetches' chorus
48 That ship
52 Zodiac sign
55 More uncanny
56 Occur before
57 Kitty on old game shows
58 HBO alternative
59 Dangerous cetacean
60 Pivotal
61 Hand-me-downs?
63 Hotelier Harry's wife
65 Writer Sarah ___ Jewett
66 Name on lifts
67 It's taken in H.S.
69 Vaporizer filler
70 Tony
71 Dolly's last name in "Hello, Dolly!"
72 False claim
77 Action sites
79 Stews aloud
80 Israeli president Weizmann
81 Girl's name on cookies
82 Anne of *Wag the Dog*
83 What ranchers drive
88 Neutral shade
90 Like much folklore
91 Theater section
92 Bass offerings
94 School setting
96 One in the sales biz
97 Crafty
98 "Jingle Bells" line starter

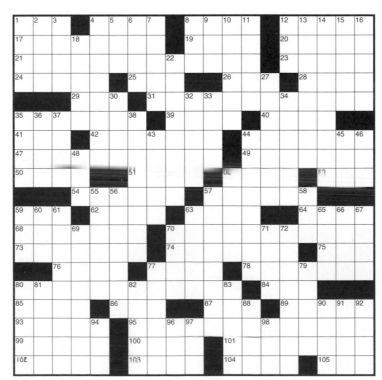

ANSWER, PAGE 93

THE WORKS!

That's all, folks

ACROSS

1 Astronomical candy company
5 For the bees
10 Make fit for *Fitness*
14 Astro Moises
15 Singer Apple
16 Itches
17 See 62-Down
19 Grasso in gubernatorial history
20 Take a fresh-air break
21 Smash into shards
23 Pale purple
25 They're described as red or white
26 Boutonniere spot
29 Sponsorship
32 Australia's national bird
33 See 62-Down
39 Julie Harris's *East of Eden* role
41 Figure-flattering fashion
42 Monopoly playing piece
43 See 62-Down
46 AP or Reuters alternative
47 Kind of blazer?
48 *The Age of Anxiety* poet
50 Jug band instrument
53 Makes uniform
56 Slates
59 Consumed matter, in medicalese
63 Madras dress
64 See 62-Down
66 Grandson of Adam
67 Modify
68 Negate, in word processing menus
69 Beer-brewing ingredient
70 Theater of Gilbert and Sullivan fame
71 Warsaw province's capital

DOWN

1 Large-scale
2 Leave ___ to be desired
3 Womanizer
4 Easily bent
5 Run ___ of (conflict with)
6 Christopher Columbus caravel
7 Red letters?
8 Crawlers on crumbs
9 Part of rock's CSNY
10 Optometrists give them
11 Mekong or Nile feature
12 Small bay
13 Autocrats
18 Struggles
22 *Lucky Jim* author Kingsley
24 Impressionist Pissarro
26 Item on Canada's flag
27 Both: Prefix
28 Manx "thanks"
30 Site of Vulcan's forges
31 Takes off
34 Rye "Bye!"
35 *The Time Machine* tribe
36 Barak who succeeded Netanyahu
37 1948 Hitchcock title
38 Teutonic turndown
40 Wow
44 Walked heavily
45 Dance with dips
49 Handy
50 Casey of Top 40 countdowns
51 Capital of Guam
52 Two from 100?
54 Blockbuster rental
55 Log piece
57 Sounds of enlightenment
58 *Once and Again* star Ward
60 Start for gram or buoy
61 Sondheim's "Sweeney"
62 Theme of this puzzle
65 Rugged wheels

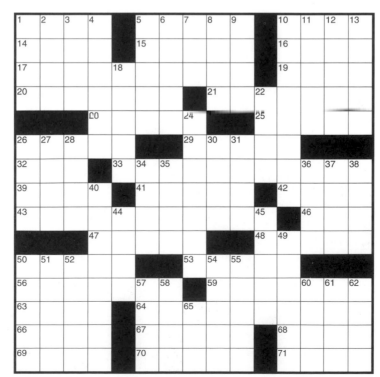

ANSWER, PAGE 95

COMBINING REFORMS

O, say can't you see?

ACROSS

1 It's a fact
6 Endure under stress
12 Doorway perpendicular
16 "I Still See ___" (*Paint Your Wagon* song)
17 Cryptic
18 Inter ___
19 *Blazing Saddles* feature?
21 Languish
22 End in the soup?
23 Fill to capacity
25 Hackberry, e.g.
26 Former Defense secretary Aspin
28 Passion for nerds?
30 Straw user's procedure?
35 *Hedda Gabler* playwright
36 Kirkuk's country
37 Awesome
38 Fringe
40 Time in the life of a Bobbsey twin?
43 Woodworker's notch
47 Flight board abbr.
48 Ryne's nine
49 Richard of *Pretty Woman*
50 Was ahead
51 Birthplace of grunge rock
53 Legal measures?
55 "My mistake!"
56 Pulitzer biographer ___ Winslow

57 At any ___
58 Class
61 Kind of school for rationalists?
64 Muckraking trail?
67 "Drop" in the gene pool
68 Iron-pumper's pride
69 Invent
70 Cough, in medicalese
75 Jazz duet
77 One who's inflicting pain with no gain?
81 Start of a conclusion
82 Cabinet department since 1977
83 City near Leipzig

84 Pack
85 "Letters From Maine" poet May
86 Little hooter

DOWN

1 Showroom model
2 Author Haley
3 Tip
4 Letters on govt.-approved meat
5 Henner of *Taxi*
6 Impact sound
7 Roaring Twenties, e.g.
8 Bit of showbiz
9 Cereal fruit
10 Use a church key
11 Nudniks

12 Pliers part
13 Sci-fi invaders
14 Barker in the White House in the 1990s
15 Ride the West and Keaton
20 Novelist Waugh
24 She's fled for political reasons
27 Disco flashers
28 Censured senator of 1967
29 Help in holdups
30 Bank holdups
31 Incensed
32 Zoo bamboo-eater
33 Cousins of rects.
34 Fleming and others

38 With 73-Down, "The Old Sod"
39 Quad building
41 Abnormally situated
42 See 59-Down
44 Intestinal adjective
45 Sealy competitor
46 Citation, Ranger, Pacer, or Corsair
49 Beaufort scale category
52 Hype
53 Atomic structure theorist Niels
54 Prefix with nucleotide
58 Brushes
59 With 42-Down, *I Spy* star
60 Cooperstown's lake
61 McDonald's : McNugget :: Burger King : ___
62 Word after catch or latch
63 Pampas cowboy
65 Sheds
66 Tropical vine
71 *Rich Man, Poor Man* author
72 Window base
73 See 38-Down
74 Opposite of dele
76 Boar bearer
78 *The A-Team* star
79 In the past
80 Thesaurus entry: Abbr.

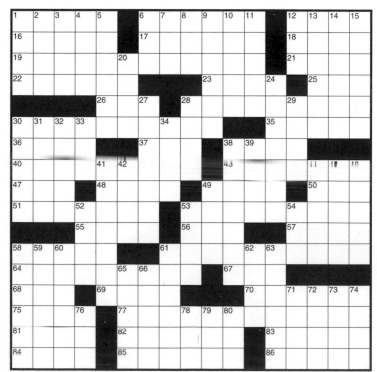

ANSWER, PAGE 81

ALPINE SCHEMING

It's all downhill from here

ACROSS

1 Do Alpine skiing, e.g.
6 Where the majority of us live
10 Love god
14 Milo in movies
15 Ski resort spots
16 Gulf of Finland feeder
17 Service for skiers?
19 Echoic negative
20 Tessellated pattern
21 "Pshaw!"
22 Bamako's country
23 Ski lodge entree?
26 Esteemed musician
30 Autocrat
31 Skilled
32 Emulate Pac-Man
34 Brazilian port
38 Skilled skiers?
42 Show awe
43 Tout's offering
44 File command
45 It's often hit at night
48 Soda brand lineup
50 Skiers' hot drinks?
54 Biz bigwig
55 Abbr. re finance charges
56 Capital of Madhya Pradesh
61 Semicolon, in emoticons
62 Ski drama?
64 Falco on *The Sporanos*
65 File command
66 Amber is one
67 Caribou, e.g.
68 Freshly
69 School for Stendhal

DOWN

1 World: Suffix
2 Christiania, today
3 Discovery sounds
4 Emmy winner Ward
5 Chinese follower of "The Way"
6 Goal
7 Bollixed-up situation
8 More than demand
9 Evaluate
10 Itemizes
11 Physiatrist's field, briefly
12 Tiny eggs
13 Colonial India's "sir"
18 Joel of *The Palm Beach Story*
24 It may form on pumpkins
25 *Critique of Pure Reason* author
26 Tatamis
27 Pitch in with sin
28 Actress Raines
29 Summer-weight fabric
33 Box off. buy
35 Wording
36 Oratorio bit
37 Mil. troop carrier
39 Samp, for example
40 Essence
41 Young man of ancient Greece
46 Like some felonies
47 TV "Kotter Gabe
49 On the beach
50 Begged for tuna, perhaps
51 Compound such as CO
52 He was blue in Disney's *Aladdin*
53 Hidden find
57 Cartel with Vienna HQ
58 100-centavo unit
59 Bittersweet's seed cover
60 Speed-swimmer's course
63 Where a layperson sits

ANSWER, PAGE 83

ONSET
Eleven "on-liners"

ACROSS

1 Sewing machine inventor
5 C's rg
9 Ansate cross
13 Downs of Derby fame
18 October birthstone
19 Steep
20 Columnar category
22 Elissa in *The Count of Monte Cristo*
23 Nintendo competitor
24 Clip, for a ship
25 Aerodynamic force at the ballpark?
27 Trudge
29 Stand under speakers
31 Jerk
32 This has one
33 Jorge or Jose lead-in
34 Sight at one author's picnic?
37 Coops
38 Grace count
40 Kosugi of Ninja films
41 Parenthetical line
43 College official
45 Protective ditch
48 Krupp works city
52 Result of cruise passes dropping overboard?
55 Rhetorical rebuke
57 Sooner migrant
58 Former Cambodian leader Lon ___
59 Chiropter, having landed at the cosmetics counter?
61 Caldecott winner Maurice
64 Neighbor of Ricky and Lucy
66 Words after *The Egg* or *The King*
67 *The ___ Squad*
68 Moon vehicle squashing the dessert?
72 Jamaican-style music
75 Pope, 440–461
76 Eye signal
77 ROY G. BIV producers
82 Woodpile atop a *mer*-colored tarp?
86 Got to glow
87 Air conditioner label abbr.
88 So-so series
89 Wading bird with a dairy addiction?
94 Kind of park
95 Adrenaline stimulus
96 Having a crest
97 ___ donna
100 Grain in some soaps
103 They're standard
104 Things piled, on floors
107 What one actor might get when digging?
111 Suffix meaning "resembling"
114 Take advantage of
115 Half of a *Star Wars* character
116 "The Big ___" (New Orleans)
117 Fran Drescher played one
119 Dog over his meat dish?
123 ___ arms
125 Noted fictional detective
126 Bread item that's boiled, then baked
127 *Steppenwolf* author
128 Japanese soup ingredient
129 Kidder's *Superman* role
130 Like a stag party-goer
131 It's a bit controlling?
132 *Vier* doubled
133 Sport ___ (rugged vehicles)

DOWN

1 Parasites' sites
2 Field of Pasta and Melba
3 Traveling joker, perhaps?
4 Jack in oaters
5 African reptile
6 A driver passes it
7 Cola's cousin
8 Airborne gaggles
9 Facilitator
10 Like Thor and Odin
11 Special skill
12 Snobbish
13 Pixie
14 Roommate, often
15 Derogatory
16 Nickel finish
17 Atomizes
21 Singer Perry and others
26 ___ Sad (city on the Danube)
28 "Virus" prefix meaning small
30 U.
35 Car gas?
36 Computer key
37 Basil-based sauce
39 Rinsed, as a car
42 Belittler
43 Chinese pooch, for short
44 Supper saver
46 Horse-wagerer's outlet
47 Al Jolson's real first name
49 ___ *cuique* (to each his own)
50 Conclusion starter
51 Scholarship basis
52 "Mayday!"
53 Toe woe
54 Hall of Fame umpire Bill, "The Old Arbitrator"
55 Yearn
56 Come to a finish
60 Summer shirt
62 Omnipresent
63 New Hampshire college city
65 Drops on the ground?
69 Swarms
70 Brook
71 The "C" in CD-ROM, e.g.

72 Kilt wearer
73 New York mayor Ed
74 Funnyman Johnson of *Laugh-In*
78 Letter-shaped girder
79 Result of a proofreader marking a bowler?

80 Mythical ennead member
81 Compass pt.
83 Stops the vibration of
84 Suffix akin to "-speak"
85 Actress Hagen
90 Decrease?
91 Somewhat silly
92 Dolt

93 Marsh wader
95 Less close
98 Model/actress from Somalia
99 *Little Women* family name
101 Homer Simpson's pop
102 Shocking experience
104 Lesson from Arthur Murray

105 Bar order, with "the"
106 Very beginning
108 Relaxed, fit-wise
109 Britney Spears's "___ Did It Again"
110 Meat garnish
112 Foolish
113 Force units

118 Org. that fights for rights
120 Goal for some Olympians
121 Lego inventor ___ Kirk Christiansen
122 One of a D.C. 100
124 Part of NIMBY

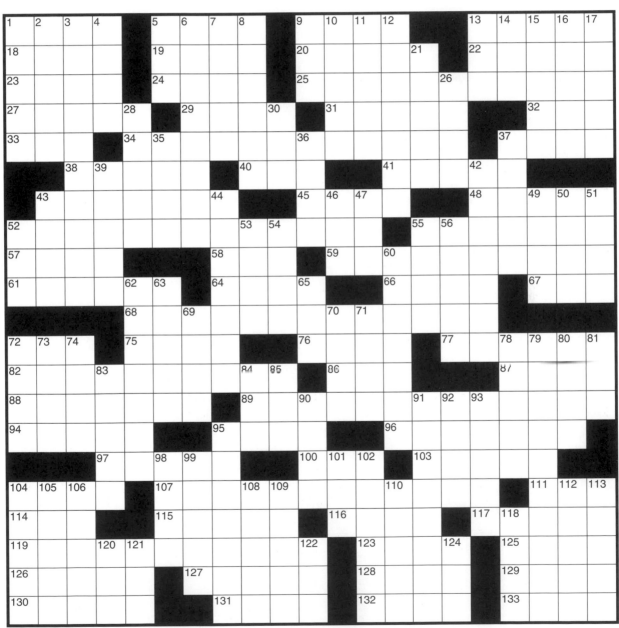

VERY-ATIONS
An extreme sport of a sort

ACROSS
1 Starters of star wars
5 Suppress
9 Canine
14 Crafty
15 Trilaminar treat
16 Biathlon need
17 Many a wedding?
19 1966 Michael Caine title role
20 Bart, Belle, and Kenneth
21 Scandinavian deity
23 Its symbol shares the 7 key
24 Hoax
26 Flaky coverings ...
28 ... and parts shaped like them
31 See 27-Down
32 EEC part
33 Fruit that's seen better days?
38 Unaffectedness
40 "Rubber Ball" singer Bobby
41 Brand of razor

42 It just won't get off the ground?
47 Sea dog
48 Spray container?
49 Nonhuman music player
51 Lascivious lads
54 Nolan Ryan was one
55 Abbr. on Aim tubes
56 Perform perfectly
58 Pay before play
62 Café cup
64 Slapstick movie?
66 Personal prefix
67 Four-ring car company

68 ___ and the Howlers (blues group)
69 "The Highwayman" poet
70 Prince Williams's alma mater
71 Act that makes Dad mad

DOWN
1 Vestibule sites
2 Pluck
3 Twice tetra-
4 Helper in the Himalayas
5 Like some flooding
6 Joe holder
7 Mil. sneak peak

8 "Hopalong Cassidy" William
9 Reindeer name
10 Kind of cloth
11 With 53-Down, garbage-eater's treat?
12 Country singer Patsy
13 Minds
18 Addams Family's Uncle Fester ___
22 What ":" may mean
25 Artist's life works
27 With 31-Across, Nana portrayer in Nana

28 Get past a seal
29 Kind of analysis: Abbr.
30 Bear, Caesarean-style
31 Wins by a landslide
34 Door word
35 Palindromic emperor
36 Caspian Sea feeder
37 Fitzgerald in Sirens
39 A deadly sin
43 Work force
44 Thessalian peak
45 Stimulant trademark
46 They "travel" on shuttles
50 Inkling
51 Paint finish type
52 Title town in a 1944 novel
53 See 11-Down
54 Rat Islands native
57 "Of wrath," in a requiem
59 Sesame Street regular
60 ___ Bator
61 Technical starter
63 Perceive
65 Tokyo, once

ANSWER, PAGE 87

THE TAMING OF THE DO
Talk about a bad hair day!

ACROSS

1 Do a base thing
6 Late bloomer
11 Poet's "field"
14 Sailed into a sandbank
16 Lean
17 "-ical" wd., e.g.
18 Start of a quote
20 Estuary
21 Sociologist's subject
22 See 48-Across
23 Birling contestant
25 Opposed, for some
26 "Your Majesty" alternative
27 An ark may hold it
28 Snag
29 Part 2 of the quote
33 *Guys and Dolls* guy Detroit
35 Tries for people food
36 It may be black or green
37 Facetious laugh syllable
38 The Lord, in Lourdes
40 Shirt collar insert
41 Part 3 of the quote
46 Letters on a cross
47 Prohibitionists

48 With 22-Across, Velvet Underground vocalist
49 Em follower?
50 Biblical twin
52 Having a smell
55 End of the quote
59 Word woven in Charlotte's web
61 Legendary birthplace of Apollo
62 Top-selling depilatory brand
63 Amounted (to)
64 Airhead
66 In good enough shape for
67 Biota component
68 *Louis le Debonnaire*, for one

69 Speaker of the quote
72 Minerva's symbol
73 Actress Owen in *Intolerance*
74 Like some seals
75 Sidekick
76 Bacon or Lamb product
77 Outplays

DOWN

1 Small game piece?
2 Big name in computers
3 Jackson's first secretary of war
4 *Heidi* setting
5 A Grant, or a Grant's rival
6 Way to fall
7 Expedited
8 Epithet
9 Presently, in the past
10 Ripostes
11 Relatively slow, as tempos go
12 Actress McClurg
13 Open, just
14 Stigmatize
15 Gray in a Wilde title
19 Subject of an APB
24 School of whales
26 Catch
27 Rush hour headache
29 Melvillean megalomaniac
30 Follows
31 Close

32 Scotland's longest river
34 Baht spender
38 Wheat used in pasta
39 Tranquil trailer
40 Stigmatize
41 From square one
42 Monotonous routine
43 "Dilbert" creator Scott
44 Birch family member
45 Cross
46 Here, to Henri
50 Overshadow
51 Comforts
52 Futile
53 Ornamental shoulder piece
54 Lack of clarity
56 Make a slip
57 Live, as a baseball
58 *Mon Oncle* actor Jacques
60 They get engaged in cars
63 Jack-in-the-pulpit cousin
64 Omit
65 Buffalo Bill's home state
66 Bone under a watch
67 Ardor
70 Thumbs-up
71 Baby dollop

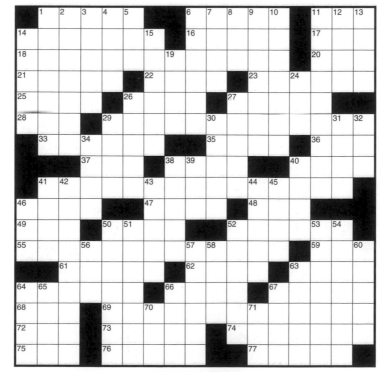

ANSWER, PAGE 89

ABSOLUTELY BUSHED

Can-do responses à la George W.

ACROSS

1 Buster of Flash Gordon fame
7 Hoopster also known as "the Big 18-wheeler"
11 Shetland girl
15 Some of life's twists
16 Forbidden: Var.
17 Radiate
18 Grouch's request?
21 Bit of gossip
22 City on the Danube
23 Punster's base
24 Openings at the weather bureau?
29 Mind
30 Taanith Esther's month
31 Does lacework
35 Turkish pooh-bah
38 "The Entertainer," for one
40 Largest of the Balearic Islands
42 Buns of Steel workout goal?
46 Matter, to a lawyer
47 Casablanca cafe
48 Informal memo heading
49 Nutmeg coverings
51 Be nosy
52 Good news from the doc?
57 Kind of heart, in song

59 Dewar's overdoer
60 Elliot who sang "It's Getting Better"
61 Ow
62 Deuce twosome
65 River rising in the Bernese Alps
67 Dress that's open?
73 Edison's ___ Park
76 Good at bar mitzvahs?
77 Birling contest
78 "Let's bring back the Spanish Inquisition," e.g.?

83 Kind of check
84 Sole
85 Rather unkind
86 Car engine attachment
87 Swear
88 Gizmo

DOWN

1 Hag
2 Historic town near Málaga
3 Like some swimmer-protection devices
4 Hallux
5 Bonnet item
6 Cornerstone abbr.
7 A Streetcar Named Desire character
8 Hurt

9 They may be involved in a crunch
10 What's what, to Caesar
11 Results in
12 Both, for a start
13 Rural skyline prominence
14 Originate
15 Union pledges
19 Andy Capp hangout
20 Beak
25 Geek
26 Leading man
27 Part of a frame
28 Tough test
32 It's up in Mexico
33 Important immune system lymphocytes
34 Gets smart

35 Rum-like beverage from Asia
36 Dancer
37 Webmaster's worry
39 Talent
41 Painter Corot or Millet
43 "___ happens ..."
44 Whiskey ingredient
45 Is shown on TV
50 Like crowds at Churchill Downs
53 Valet's income
54 Beauty salon sound
55 Biblical kingdom
56 Like some type: Abbr.
58 All-star, e.g.
63 Mountain climbers' spikes
64 Slingshot ammo
66 Brush up on
68 Alley ___
69 One of Frank's exes
70 What a band might cover
71 Most minute
72 Wyle of ER
73 Become engaged
74 Fair
75 Cpl. and Sgt.
79 Antique restorer's skill, for short
80 Letters in a pot
81 German car
82 Gift of flowers

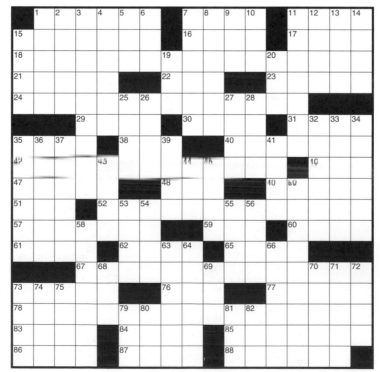

ANSWER, PAGE 91

KNOCK IT OFF!
Just don't knock it

ACROSS

1 Swindle
5 Lucretia in women's rights history
9 Renoir, the film director
13 Circumference ÷ diameter ratios
16 Elster Olsona's successor
17 Piece for Cecilia Bartoli
18 Moises Alou was one
19 Kind of card
20 It's "knocked off" in fights
22 It's "knocked off" at college
24 Talk show host Williams
25 Principle
27 Jordan's only seaport
28 Porridge ingredient
29 Pro ___ (proportionally)
30 Sight
33 Slangy mouth
34 It's "knocked off" during business deals
38 Sight
42 Disney CEO Michael
43 Butter sub
44 Venezuela's capital
46 Hoopster Thurmond
48 Naught, in Minorca
52 It's sitting on top of the world
53 Even under ideal conditions
56 Got a bod impression
57 Bit of cheer?
58 It's "knocked off" at offices
61 Advent's end
62 Roman magistrate
64 Surfer's handful
65 Appetite enhancers
67 Overhaul
68 Grate upon
69 Stewing
70 Problem
72 Going out, in a way
76 White is one kind
77 They're "knocked off" by clothiers
82 Worldwide workers' org.
83 Fiend
84 Many
85 Barbecue site
90 Heliacal
92 Resided
94 Place for changing
95 He's "knocked off" in some movies
98 They're "knocked off" by wondrous feats
100 Intentions
101 Mythical monsters
102 Plotting
103 Mean
104 Pre-O trio
105 Marks of Zorro
106 Speak weakly
107 Intro French verb

DOWN

1 Jazzy dance
2 Dugout, e.g.
3 Fight site
4 They're rigged
5 It often has stories of stores
6 Gold, in Montana's motto
7 Popular breath mints
8 Have a break
9 Leap in *Coppelia*
10 Devon's capital
11 Earth Day mo.
12 Brief case?
13 Melon-like fruit
14 Pain reliever, maybe
15 *Hombre*'s wrap
19 Web site info source
21 Page, nowadays
23 Big Band singer Freda
26 Occiput's neighbor
29 Journalist/reformer Jacob
31 Soprano Renata
32 Brazilian "King of Soccer"
35 Attain
36 Julio Gallo's partner in wine
37 Chinese secret society
38 "Boo!" sayer, e.g.
39 Moving holiday event
40 Corsage flower
41 Feline, to Tweety Pie
45 Mention
47 "... trespasses ___ forgive ..."
49 Citadel graduate, perhaps
50 Get more than sidetracked
51 Latin carol starter
53 Humorist George and kin
54 Packed firmly
55 "We're not providing," on invites
56 Edible cousin of cotton
59 It has a delete function
60 Wander about
63 City near Milan
66 CIA forerunner
68 Band at weddings
69 Research facility: Abbr.
71 Where Greeks assembled
73 Hebridean hillside
74 Go ___ (fail)
75 One of related element forms
77 Anatomically terminal
78 God, in some Hebrew texts
79 Grave
80 Knock off pounds
81 Places for losers?
86 Overhead
87 Unspoken
88 Type of loom
89 Stops for desert refreshment
91 Sit-ups strengthen them
93 *Swiss Family Robinson* author
94 It's often dusted
96 Days of Xmas, e.g.
97 Advanced deg.-seeker's test
99 Beehive State athlete

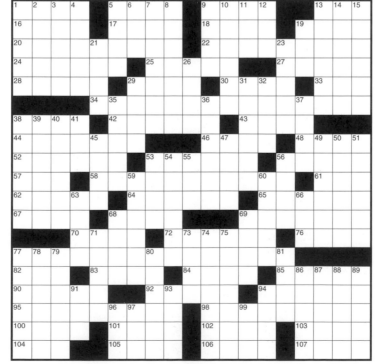

ANSWER, PAGE 93

MR. HOLLAND'S OPUS

To blow the windmills of your mind

ACROSS

1 Doorway vertical
5 Bruce Bondeitner role of 1982
9 Those, re *señoras*
13 Nebbish
18 Fancy product
19 Movement to meles
20 Cushy jobs, e.g.
22 Iman's pre-actress job
23 MR. HOLLAND, WHY ARE YOU IN THE CITY?
26 Extant
27 Certain beneficiary
28 Once more
29 Kind of shark
31 Poet Hughes
32 Wood rods
35 Ill. neighbor
36 Iona College team
38 Dance partner?
39 "Gross!"
40 HOW DO YOU LIKE THE FOOD?
44 Fragrant bloomers from China
46 Stewed
47 Stemmed
48 Mythical Himalayan monster
49 WHERE ARE YOU FROM, ORIGINALLY?
54 Monetary unit of the Mideast
57 Perseveres
58 Island birthplace of Pythagoras
62 Being sans pigment
64 Prohibition opponents
65 AAA recommendation
67 Famed trial judge
68 With 70-Across, WHAT'S IN THAT BOX YOU'VE GOT?
70 See 68-Across
74 ___ Miss
75 Holland is on the North one
76 Scale notes
77 Rich pastries
78 Pine family member
81 Steak knife challenge
84 Storage or stopping place
85 HOW WOULD YOU DESCRIBE THE LOCAL ATM?
88 What *la lune* lights up
91 Town, Scottish-style
93 Patient care provider: Abbr.
94 Small mosaic piece
97 WHAT'S YOUR FAVORITE ART FILM?
102 El Al destination: Abbr.
103 Poaching targets
104 Rage
105 Goatling's cry
106 Stewing
108 Lyon who played 1962's *Lolita*
109 One of the Near Islands
110 Oversupply
112 Peeper, e.g.
113 Kind of wave
115 WHY IS YOUR SON HERE SO QUIET?
121 Get the beau on the road?
122 Porter alternative
123 Quattro maker
124 NYC neighborhood
125 Body shop jobs
126 Shelley output
127 Loudly colored
128 Pay attention to

DOWN

1 Skippy rival
2 Bother
3 Debussy's sea
4 Soak oneself
5 Believers of sorts
6 Essen basin
7 Motor ending, commercially
8 1998 Olympics site
9 It's thrust at Olympics
10 Snail-like
11 ___ *Wiedersehen*
12 Reacted warmly
13 Certain Fed
14 Night bird, à la Milne
15 Staff of *Life*
16 Income
17 Hazing victim, often
21 Ancient Roman dress
24 Sun: Prefix
25 Annul
30 Comparatively vile
32 Obligation
33 Curvy molding
34 ANYTHING TO SAY ABOUT YOUR COLONIAL ANCESTOR?
35 "___ girl!"
37 Cabs, vans, etc.
38 Mouth-like opening
41 Dreamcast maker
42 Hidden valleys
43 Historic stretches
45 Unyielding
50 Stat start
51 Trail mix fruit
52 Y intersections
53 Duck, in Dresden
55 Word before horse or track
56 Baseball's Darling and Guidry
59 WHAT'S THAT "POTTED" PLANT YOU'RE NURSING ALONG?
60 Its seat is Nebraska City
61 Propagates
62 Skipping the service
63 1970 Kinks hit
64 Mooring spot
66 Cigar tip?
69 Utah's lily

70 Lounge (about)
71 ___ *Three Lives* (1950s TV series)
72 "Alley ___"
73 Danish dough
76 Be tight
79 Some underground stems
80 Titanic

82 Snow place like home?
83 Very sticky stuff
84 Thuringian three
86 Poaching, e.g.
87 Highest active volcano in Europe
89 Actress Von Glatz

90 Lemony, maybe
91 Deceive
92 Prodded
95 Adds, as to batter
96 Church group
97 Firmly established
98 Kin of "The Sultan of Swat"

99 Words with one's word
100 Ratite meat sources
101 Porch furniture material
107 Spurting
109 Publican's offerings
111 Developer's purchases

112 Name of many a pooch
114 Inclined
116 Turf
117 Shade
118 Water temperature tester
119 Fidel's helpmate
120 Coal carrier

INITIAL REACTION
Phrases with something in common

ACROSS

1 Bumpkin
6 Cone contents
12 L squared
15 Miss equivalent?
16 Participating in drunken revelry
17 Item sometimes called a spoon
18 Twist away
19 Posh nestling place
21 Like some Internet interviews
23 "... pudding ___ the eating"
24 Thwart
25 Rank, in Rouen
27 Fray
31 Undesirable fruit trait
34 Sportscaster also known as "The Mouth"
35 "Start the film!"
36 Nordic flyer
37 Gandhi's tongue
38 Omens
40 Oft-initialized e-mail phrase
44 Partridge's family member
45 Martinelli and Lanchester
47 Title for G.B.S.'s Warren
50 Joint projections

51 London's ___ Garden
52 18th-century French dances
54 It may involve hives
55 Fictional youth-sleuths Frank and Joe
56 Desert-like
57 Blue dye source
58 Butter brand
64 1976 Spinners hit
68 Ere
69 Stretch (out)
70 An anticoagulant
71 Bagpipe pipe
72 N.Y.'s Clinton, e.g.
73 Howie of *St. Elsewhere*
74 Burdened, in a way

DOWN

1 Ketch-like boat
2 Biblical Ahab's father
3 Chicken-cooking style
4 Something ___ (a lulu)
5 Sentence leniently
6 Gastropod for gastronomes
7 ___ Crunch (Quaker Oats cereal)
8 Oklahoma Indian
9 Pained expression, in comics
10 Campaign figure
11 Good name for a cook

12 Hair goos
13 Actress Ribisi
14 Cause of chapping
16 North of Virginia
20 Chinese capital of 11 dynasties
22 Football Hall of Fame coach Chuck
25 Dirty Harry portrayer
26 Type in a Jan and Dean title
27 Soph. spot
28 Many a spring
29 Annapolis inst.
30 Disgusted
31 American-breed horses
32 Singers John and Britt

33 Unimak islander
35 Name on lighters
38 "Shh," for Schubert
39 Do (the math)
41 Hose parts
42 Friendly introduction?
43 Mild oath
46 Shoat cote
47 ___ *Navy* (Borgnine sitcom)
48 Virginia city in the Blue Ridge range
49 Done one's best
51 Muse of history
53 Thumb-twiddling
54 Enoch of Tennyson title
56 Incus
58 Its symbol is Pb
59 Interlaken's canalized river
60 High-profile do
61 Crackpot
62 River of Northern Ireland
63 It's a start
65 Physicist Georg
66 Stephen of *Angie*
67 TLC provider

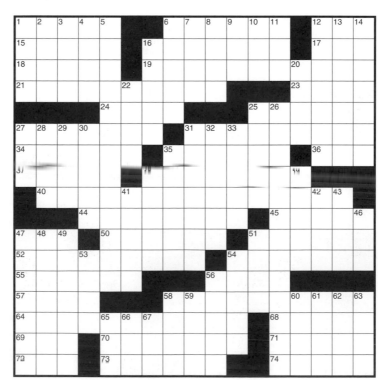

SKIP THE ER RERUNS

But not the originals

ACROSS

1 Swiss-French mountain range
5 Omar of *Scream 2*
9 Temperate
14 Annoys
15 Yorkshire river
16 Boorish
17 It comes from a Daisy air rifle?
19 Own
20 Dahl or Francis
21 Pollster Elmo
22 Grant (us), in the *Agnus Dei*
24 Aunt who wrote a *Cope Book*
26 That, at the Alhambra
27 Legend end
28 Ella's forte
31 Word for "wd."
33 She takes one under her wing?
36 Memo "pronto"
39 Sault Sainte Marie's province
40 Hyundai model
42 Wind instrument

43 Dangerous herb?
45 Pace
47 Russell's role in *Tombstone*
48 Gamma counterpart, position-wise
49 Grampus
51 Indian nursemaid
53 Lodge group
55 Bugs, the crime boss
57 Like long, tiresome meetings
60 Way to be taken
61 Bunk in the mail?
65 Recess
66 Buck's tail?

67 The Hawkeye State
68 Wet, as a stamp pad
69 Doctrines
70 Bean Town team player

DOWN

1 Peter Pan rival
2 Letters re links
3 *King Kong* movie co.
4 Egyptian city on the Nile
5 Jazz pianist Hines
6 Wind instrument
7 Is ___ (likely will)
8 Ed Norton's workplace

9 June bug or dung beetle
10 Latin word on the back of a one-dollar bill
11 Cue for a kind of pool?
12 McClurg and Falco
13 Kind of dressing
18 Item worn by math homework doers?
22 Boring sound
23 Way into a bivalve?
25 *Resurrection* symphony composer
27 Get an ___ effort

29 Down Under "Dang!"
30 French possessive
32 Parade marchers
34 "Voilà!"
35 Anatomical tissue layer
37 Van Gogh's *Bedroom at ___*
38 Ale type
41 Lanvin perfume since 1927
44 Broadcaster Jim and satirist Tom
46 Lit
49 Muscat native
50 Sign of spring
52 One of Grover's veeps
54 Song-like
56 Reason to take Aleve
58 Minute thing
59 Pontiacs of yore
62 *The Gold Bug* writer
63 It does the hole thing for you
64 Butter portion

ANSWER, PAGE 83

HOW DAFFY!
Ducky, too

ACROSS

1 Wild
6 ___ the Covenant
11 Starry
17 They may be therapeutic
19 Puffy bread of India
20 Punjab capital
21 Baby genius?
23 One with a mortgage
24 Martha Stewart concern
25 Unpopular trait at a nudist colony?
27 Consumes
29 Titanic, as movies may be
31 Temple
32 Tolkien's Treebeard tribe
33 Variety show makeup
35 Agglomeration
38 Bugs pursuer
40 Shriveled folks in a comics kingdom?
45 Article in Aragón
48 Samantha's *Bewitched* cousin
49 Hokkaido industrial city
50 Sir Hillary achievement
52 Pearl Mosque site
54 Emulate Flo-Jo
56 Dodeca-, less four
57 How the pulmonary patient passed his exam?
64 Broadway Rose-lover
65 Copy cats, in a way
66 TV tec Peter
67 Lip-like edge
70 It may be skipped
73 Library area
77 Memo header's letters
78 Machine-made snack bit?
81 Lived
82 Famed Laker, familiarly
83 Shoppers' magnet
84 Month of Purim
87 Disapproving sounds
90 Gang's domain
93 Carry in a wagon, say
94 Group rate for church?
98 Lofty nest
100 Henry Clay, for one
101 Make it big as a belly dancer?
105 Go back on one's word
106 Psych suffix
107 Guarantee
108 Cleaned some boards
109 Clean some boards
110 Snake venom, e.g.

DOWN

1 Colgate detergent
2 Be off
3 Old-fashioned open car
4 Friend Nancy, in Nancy
5 Thrusting weapon
6 Parrot
7 Campus mil. group
8 Long-time German chancellor
9 Droxies' look-alikes
10 Estuary
11 "Praise the Lord!"
12 Just-mentioned
13 Like some parks or parties
14 1998 film directed by John Frankenheimer
15 Don't exist
16 City on the Aire
18 End
22 Film director von Stroheim
26 State of resentment
27 Derbies, e.g.
28 Overdoer's problem
30 *ER* character Dr. Finch
34 Oath-taker
36 Under-the-table tidbit
37 Flow of woe
39 Canine fixer's deg.
41 *Picnic* playwright
42 Twelve Oaks neighbor
43 "Phooey!"
44 Smart response?
45 Peace Nobelist before Desmond
46 Part of ABM
47 Baseball card fig.
51 Courvoisier, Otard, etc.
53 Key nucleotide in energy processes
55 Work measurement unit
57 Mast or past preceder
58 Internet auction site
59 Andersson of Bergman movies
60 Stillness
61 Ziegfeld Follies costume designer
62 Boot
63 Proverbs preposition
68 Suffix with glob or vein
69 Like many a saint
71 Japanese drama form
72 "L'___, c'est moi": Louis XIV
74 Bordeaux estates
75 1,000 grams, for short
76 Flow like shaken colas
79 Dry run
80 Waters of old Rome
81 Pens
84 Earlier than, in poetry
85 Bold one
86 Whirlpool rival
88 Hairy fruit
89 Last thing?
91 Anatomical network
92 Bow
95 Orchestra neighbor
96 Noted sex researcher
97 Evian existence
99 In that case
102 Prefix meaning "below"
103 CAT scan alternative
104 Bard's contraction

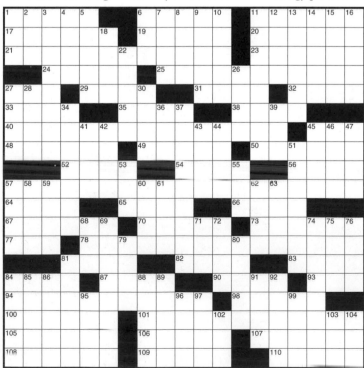

ANSWER, PAGE 85

SUSS OUT SEUSS
With apologies to a favorite Dr.

ACROSS

1 Pats (down)
6 Stroller in Covent Garden
10 Gabon president ___ Bongo
14 1960s painting genre
15 Draw, say, a music staff
16 Home of the rumba
17 Seuss being's outline?
20 Like some salons
21 Unlike old bathtubs
22 Festoon
24 Kanga's kid, in a Milne story
25 Christmas season, for a Seuss character?
32 Pea family member
33 Train
34 Thick slice
35 Paul Newman film hit of 1963
36 General on Chinese menus

37 Mountain in Homeric legend
38 Forever, seemingly
40 Ancient wrap akin to a chiton
42 Overcook
43 Johnny Mercer song to a Seuss animal?
46 Charlotte, TV's "Mrs. Garrett"
47 Prunelle liqueur flavorer
48 More constricted, old-style
53 *Full House* pair
57 Got Seuss's pocket-creature started?

59 Cassini with designs on Jackie
60 Dash
61 *México* snow
62 Potato chip brand
63 Method: Abbr.
64 Some end in -on

DOWN

1 Versatile health food
2 Neat as ___
3 *Amahl and the Night Visitors* visitors
4 Realm of Frederick the Great
5 Sown

6 Part of LPGA
7 "Dennis the Menace" dog
8 Too
9 It's usually lit in December
10 Spotted cats
11 Button on a TV remote
12 *Sesame Street* subject
13 Bowl calls
18 Wrest (from)
19 School in a Thomas Gray ode title
23 Slum place
25 Overcharge
26 International golf cup
27 Kind of jar
28 Nice schools
29 Troy, to Titus

30 Parent of *niños*
31 *Personal Witness* author
32 Horse-drawn carriage
39 Puzzling
40 Rages
41 Running, in a way
42 Lombardy commune
44 Not "of the cloth"
45 Darjeeling alternative
48 Deliberate
49 Anklebones
50 "Herb of grace" and kin
51 Conger-like
52 Vitamin bottle info: Abbr.
54 ___ out a living (gets by)
55 Campbell of *Party of Five*
56 Jeanne, Bernadette, etc.: Abbr.
58 Pangolin's tidbit

ANSWER, PAGE 87

SOUTHERN-ORS
Some fine Dixie puns sure to draw "ohs" from solvers

ACROSS

1 Popular pens
5 Letters
9 Diner orders
18 Declarer
18 Slouth speaker
19 One who's quoted
20 Jacob's first wife
21 Brimless hat
22 Underdogs?
24 Clued in about
25 Circular
26 Get another turn at dice
27 Like a shaving task?
30 American artist Rembrandt
31 Tavern
32 Part of a science course
33 "Alfred" poet
34 Kvetch's favorite TV show?
41 Gob of gobs: Abbr.
42 Wannabe's model
43 Bullfight cheer
44 The "u" of yuppie
48 Exuded
51 *Three Stooges* segment?
56 Inventor Nikola
57 Kind of ad
58 Kind of head
59 Old TV actress Lansing
60 Yearn (for)
62 A/C abbr.
64 Singer Eartha
65 Pagoda bell
66 What a klutz does at the bakery?
72 It's "made over" in Holland
73 Extremely
74 WWII area: Abbr.
75 Turgenev's birthplace
76 DXLV ÷ V
77 Prefix with -morphic
78 Biting
80 French red wine
84 What cannibals set on the table?
89 Burger topper
90 A camel'd walk a mile for it
91 Writer Fleming
92 Loch that feeds Ness
94 Yang's counterpart
95 What one might get at a wiener roast?
102 ___ *poetica*
105 "___ minute ..."
106 Data: Abbr.
107 Toll plaza no-no
108 Where Humpty Dumpty should have lived?
113 It was played on a *lyra*
115 Old war story
116 Whole nine yards
117 Invitation to a treehouse?
121 Sturdy cotton
122 Country's McEntire
123 Jibe
124 Perrier and such
125 Onetime dentist's supply
126 Yemeni port
127 Part of CD-ROM
128 Deletion cancellation

DOWN

1 Woman's haircut
2 "Love ___ leave it!"
3 Southern ice cream parlor offerings?
4 Be plenty mad
5 Deceive
6 Chowed down
7 Front end?
8 Author Eda
9 Formless form
10 Filmmaker Riefenstahl
11 Tell mom, e.g.
12 Yom Kippur horn
13 Gillette product
14 "Va-va-va-___!"
15 Rig
16 Too thin, as batter
17 Papyrus is one
19 Gelatin or starch
23 Farm soil
28 Insider's talk
29 *Mikado* costume part
31 Old English folk song
34 Hat thief?
35 Douay Bible book
36 Ark builder
37 Model Carol
38 Funnyman Brooks
39 Prompted
40 Verb after "thou"
45 Popular theater name
46 In the company of
47 Nag's complaint
49 Suffix in cytology
50 Per
52 Analogy words
53 Process text
54 Process
55 Many a Wayne movie
57 Old coin of Cádiz
61 Honey spots
63 Sport ___ (modern vehicle)
64 Cheap imitation

65 Robot of Jewish folklore
66 Tropical lizard
67 Minneapolis suburb
68 Street fleet
69 Funnywoman Lebowitz
70 Alt. to underlining

71 Sample tape
77 Screening
79 *Whose Life ___ Anyway?*
81 Drama of an office heater breakdown?
82 Of the ear
83 Bop
85 Brutus's force
86 Go phfft!
87 Cuvée

88 Bit of gossip
89 Television, slangily
93 Was close friends (with)
96 "Check your ___?"
97 Turkey's capital
98 Savored
99 Like some

100 Ancient Elam's capital
101 Crees, Creeks, etc.
102 Old-womanish
103 Burning again
104 Sound of a two-pointer
109 Kind of lock
110 Command, Southern-styled

111 Alternative for Hamlet
112 Muslim call to prayer
114 Musical direction for two
118 Big: Abbr.
119 Certain kitty, for short
120 No. after a

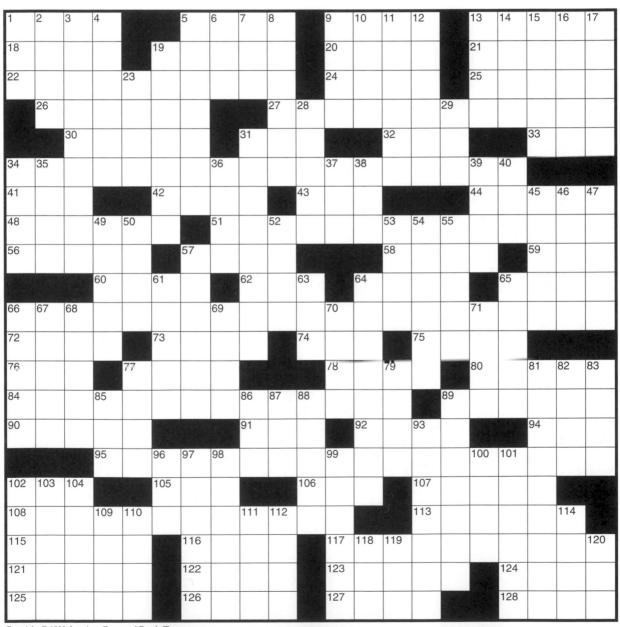

ANSWER, PAGE 89

SPACE CRAFT
An inner space adventure

ACROSS

1 Historic French region
7 Bluish-green
11 Sweet people
16 Thumbed (through)
17 Rotation
18 Miss ___ (*Dallas* matriarch)
19 C o n s e - q u e n c e
22 ___-European
23 Have the ___ for
24 Psychoanalyst Wilhelm
25 WWII arena abroad
26 Today's preferred term for Lapp
27 Confessional list
28 A p p l a u s e
35 Fall foliage assortment
36 Cat's "Scat!"
37 U.S.-Can. canal region
38 Machinate
41 Skittles partner
43 Counterpart of Helios
44 Q u a r r e l
49 Popular Net provider
50 Endure
51 Holds forth
52 Frank McCourt bestseller

53 Ending meaning lizard
55 Forbidding
56 P r e d i c t i o n
62 Ancient ointment source
63 ___ even keel
64 Fault or tee lead-in
66 Beat
68 *Alhambra*'s A-count
69 They have captives' audiences
70 I n d i g e n c e
74 Alamogordo event in '45
75 Kelp, e.g.
76 Cause bitter resentment
77 "Tiny Bubbles" singer

78 Jumper in a pocket
79 Place for a jumper

DOWN

1 1967 Dionne Warwick hit
2 Roof type
3 *La Tosca* author Victorien
4 Pick target, perhaps
5 Alphabet arc
6 Writer LeShan
7 Parlor reception
8 "Cut that out!"
9 Pots at socials
10 *Sense and Sensibility* director Lee
11 Protects
12 Sprite-like

13 Baldwin in *Beetlejuice*
14 Like Bill Gates
15 Resolute
20 Scorches
21 Some native New Yorkers
26 *Serenade* painter Jan
27 Sew gathers in rows
29 "The Family Circus" mom
30 Sport with heavy competition?
31 Fool
32 Upside trait
33 Jazz clarinetist Jimmie
34 Fools
38 Deluge
39 ___ *de Guerre* (French military award)

40 *The Planets* composer
41 Crumb catcher
42 Trib staffers
45 Attached, in a way
46 *Palm Court Bidding* penner
47 Kind of acid in gouty joints
48 Vicky Lawrence played one
53 Stops being at ease
54 Just ___ in the bucket
55 Comprehension
57 Trap with a net
58 Search for provisions
59 Like some seminars
60 Herons' cousins
61 Mosey (along)
65 Until now
66 Jazz great Puente
67 Tree of life setting
68 Prefix with phase or dynamic
69 Founder of Stoicism
70 Green roll
71 *The ___ Quartet* (Paul Scott novels)
72 Tolkien creature
73 Kilmer in films

ANSWER, PAGE 91

HONEYBUNCH
The colonial kind

ACROSS

1 Bender
4 Anatomical cavity
9 Feature of Janis Joplin's voice
13 "Yeah, right!"
15 Brilliantly colored fish
16 Cinders in old strips
17 Steak order word
18 Make shinier, maybe
19 Town on the Santa Fe Trail
20 Italian toast
22 Part of an ER caseload
24 Highlands sound
27 Hans Christian Andersen tale
30 Trouble
31 ___ Pakistan (Bangladesh, once)
32 Suspicious
36 Sends angry posts
39 "The Little Colonel" Reese
40 Common mixer
41 Commune W. of Caen

44 Actress Munson
45 Julie Harris was one in *Requiem for a Heavyweight*
49 Solving this puzzle?
52 Crossword creation step
53 Peripatetic people
57 Like an endangered *avis*
58 *Jailhouse Rock* star
61 Cool, in hip-hop
62 ___ Lacoste
63 Comedi-Anne
64 Sch. with an Albany campus

65 Bolus
66 Words with attorneys?
67 Reformer Dorothea

DOWN

1 Yaks
2 Sailing from Boothbay, say
3 Mushroom cap part
4 Precedes
5 "... when I ___ my lips, let no dog bark": Shakespeare
6 Froot Loops' toucan
7 Heptathlon event
8 On ___ (bingeing)

9 Homecoming participant
10 Spanish "poplar" mission
11 Ashcan school artist John F.
12 Out
14 Messes up
21 Turn brown bathing
23 Dancer Astaire
25 New Deal Industrial Act org.
26 Mensa fig.'s
27 One of Ohio's presidents
28 Hawaii County seat
29 Zip
33 Furry Endor dweller

34 ___ Lacoste
35 X was one
37 Gives a bum steer
38 Organic water-tainter
39 Buzzer of a sort
41 Tank top, e.g.
42 Make It
43 Legal deg.
46 Truffaut's field
47 "War on Poverty" grp.
48 Answers invites, informally
49 Backdrop curtain
50 Hotel of "Eloise" capers
51 They're now in some Monopoly banks
54 Netanyahu successor Barak
55 Royal sari-wearer
56 "Come Sail Away" rock group
59 Mother in the comic strip "Stone Soup"
60 A Gershwin

ANSWER, PAGE 93

PLAY WITH YOUR FOOD!

Don't worry, Mom won't mind

ACROSS

1 Judy Garland's first girl
5 Irises opening, e.g.
9 Colt filler
13 Erwin of old TV
16 Surrounded by
17 Quod ___ demonstrandum
18 Swedish car company
19 ___ *Sorry Now?*
20 Playable food?
23 Colt filler
24 It may be acute
25 Latin diminutive
26 Chaos
28 Playable food?
31 Fleischer, George W.'s press secretary
34 Girl in a Left Banke song
35 Land in camera history
38 Tiny opening
42 People counted on them
46 Applied sci. deg.
47 Musical eighths
48 Playable food?
51 Thingamajig
52 Singer's fifth
53 Abbr. in many Manhattan addresses
54 Buffalo, bison, etc.
55 Playable food?
59 Jacob's wombmate
62 Subject of much doting

63 "The Science Guy" Bill
64 Dixie speech features
68 Playable food?
71 More impetuous
72 Height: Prefix
73 Singer Lehmann or Lenya
74 Strasbourg's region, once
75 Pago Pago is there
77 Of course, slangily
81 Eats
82 Playable food?
89 Girlish, in an old-fashioned way
91 Words with jam or stew
92 Shoe lacer's target
96 Citrus hybrid
97 Playable food?
100 Fig is one kind
101 Legendary piper's followers
102 Greek letters
103 "Cheerio!"

104 Smidgen
105 They love leftovers
106 Force unit
107 Month before Nisan

DOWN

1 Buddhist monk
2 Colorful computer
3 Mineral in cold lozenges
4 Pit viper's cousin
5 Slugs
6 Altdorf's canton
7 Flower in the Black Forest?
8 Hot
9 Quick-wink link
10 Girl of Barry Manilow song
11 Doug Henning's art
12 More than plump
13 Spar solo
14 Schlep
15 Defunct atlas abbr.

19 Great amount
21 Go out ___ limb
22 Like erbium or terbium
27 Kind of acid in fats
29 U.S.'s C. in C.
30 True
31 No centipede, this
32 Edward G.'s *Little Caesar* role
33 Division word
36 ___ *of the Dead* (Karloff chiller)
37 Element of Las Vegas?
39 Enjoyed oneself
40 Trotter's path
41 Paved the way for
43 Hockey's Hector who is also known as "Toe"
44 Cal. notation
45 Coed academy since 1996 (with The)
48 Neil Simon nickname

49 Massey of *Balalaika*
50 Piña ___ (rum drink)
52 Attack
56 Litmus ___
57 Dancer/actress Charisse
58 Sr.'s reserves
59 Those, re *casas*
60 Grp. that runs homeless shelters
61 FedExed, perhaps
65 Part of SWAK
66 Loopy-braided film princess
67 Mmes., in Málaga
69 Make up?
70 Star that comes out late at night?
71 Echoic heckle
76 Do-___ (no-turning-back)
78 Related
79 Was inclined
80 Prone to prattle
83 Mural prefix
84 Unpolluted
85 Hilton rival
86 Don't waste
87 British novelist Barbara
88 Nostril partitions
89 Dog in Chaplin's *A Dog's Life*, e.g.
90 Pearl Mosque city
93 Heavy metal
94 Henri feminizer?
95 Past potentate
98 Balaam's rebuker
99 Conducted

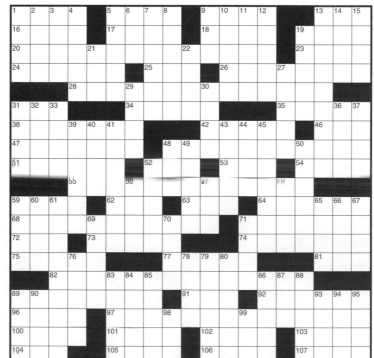

ANSWER, PAGE 95

TOPS

Some are "on the house"

ACROSS

1 Breeze-dries
5 Rounded mass
10 Register upon arrival
16 One left Hook short-handed
17 Greta Garbo's role in *The Temptress*
18 Rub off
19 Game played with a "top"?
22 *The Odd Couple* playwright
23 It's snow fun
24 Appealed, colloquially
25 Velcro stuff
27 Bear, as costs
29 "Robin ___" (Scottish ballad)
32 Jet, at Orly?
33 Nutrition guideline fig.
36 Vacation spot that's "tops"?
41 Actress Balin
42 Dance on nachos?
43 Hammerhead, maybe
44 Spanish pronoun
46 Simple shelters
50 Martinelli of *Hatari!*
51 Bizarre
53 Ace in bridge
55 Popeye, for one

56 "Top" film director?
61 Marsh
62 CCCXVII × III
63 Come to
64 Kind of card
66 Grinch-like look
69 Quarrel finished?
72 Feeling relaxed
75 Intaglio's opposite
77 "Top" classical piece?
80 Put-down
81 Sambuca flavoring
82 Flyer from Ben Gurion
83 Cooks one's goose
84 Dapper
85 Strike from *O*, e.g.

DOWN

1 Good Book book
2 Comedian Corey
3 Commodious
4 Fulbright beneficiary
5 One of an ice cream duo
6 Ransom in car history
7 Onion's kin
8 Brought to ruin
9 Wise
10 Cantina pitcherful
11 Scottish : Mac- :: Arabic : ___
12 Like some punches
13 Chem. compound in kitchens

14 Run in place
15 Financial aid criterion
20 Battery parts
21 Destined to get
26 From birth
28 Pie chart parts
30 Pennsylvania's ___, for one
31 Tabula ___
33 Theater district
34 On the back, in biology
35 Asia Minor capital
36 Close, as a balloon
37 Iffy
38 Porch furniture palm
39 Habanera descendant
40 Alternative to *café*

45 Suffix with north and south
47 Grounds for a suit
48 *Novus ___ seclorum* (Great Seal motto)
49 Amish and Mennonites, e.g.
52 Livy's "Lo!"
54 Subtle variation
57 Striking forces
58 One deadly sin
59 Hero that comes with water
60 Like some trouser fronts
64 *Concentration* puzzle
65 Elg in 1950s films
67 Rousseau title pupil
68 Nephritic
69 Foofaraw
70 Words from *SNL*'s Mr. Bill
71 City near Phoenix
73 Stewing state
74 American League division
76 Check out for pickup?
78 Computer key abbr.
79 He held reign in Spain

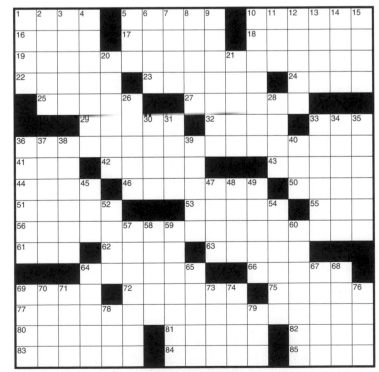

ANSWER, PAGE 81

71

ANTHROPOMORPHIC ADDITIONS

Wherein prefixes add a human element

ACROSS

1 They get broken at the table
6 Soviet workers' cooperative
11 Positive aspect
17 Cal Ripken, Frank Robinson, etc.
20 Canakry's country
22 MacNeil's former news partner
23 No sad sacks, these?
25 Dog-ear, e.g.
26 Rorschach medium
27 McClurg of *Mr. Mom*
28 Sets, say, a setter (upon)
29 Tooth crown projections
30 Metal in a stew?
35 Motif
38 Unvarying
39 More exacting
43 Cosmonaut Gagarin
44 Director Riefenstahl
46 Fault

48 Y2K follower, classically
49 Veggie with self-control?
54 Perp's charges
55 There's one on a one
56 *Tío*, in Tours
57 Unseats
58 *The Very Hungry Caterpillar* author Eric
59 Asia Minor part, once
60 Where spoons are played
61 Library section
62 Current in heaven?
67 Goes bad
68 Taken place
69 "Able" palindrome center
70 Caustic
71 Frosh, usually
73 Calculator button word
74 Cassius, to Caesar
77 Dice
78 Very blue bluebells?
81 CSA soldier

82 Vaccine developer Salk
83 French Polynesia constituents
84 Whole lot
85 Storm
87 Beep, maybe
89 Galloping gal
90 Shrinking spread?
96 Biblical patriarch
99 Seine feeder
100 Horse color
101 Earlier
104 Preparer of James Bond's martinis
106 Drink in a stupor?
110 *Corrida* figure
111 Cordwood measures
112 Pop-up item
113 Hans Christian Andersen's birthplace
114 One of the King Sisters
115 Jerks

DOWN

1 Centers of attention
2 *East of Eden* twin

3 Drop in the bucket?
4 *Barney* fan
5 Cap is one kind
6 Crop-raising, cropped
7 Citrus plants' family
8 Organ composition?
9 Naval standard
10 Parasite
11 Danube River city
12 Fan-feathered friend
13 Gotten smaller
14 Gets (one's) goat
15 Sound, as sleep
16 Drops the ball
18 *Momo* author Michael
19 Hullabaloo
21 Abbr. with prof or principal
24 Some drops
30 Drop
31 O'Connor of *Xena: Warrior Princess*
32 *Metamorphoses* poet

33 Turn forgoer's phrase
34 Famous partner
35 It's on a Rolls
36 Donald Duck nephew
37 Scottish Gaelic, once
40 Turkish inn
41 Service
42 Hiphuggers have low ones
44 Permissible
45 Zedong contemporary
46 Unit of flow volume
47 D-Con victim
50 Fixed, in a way
51 Writers Quindlen and Sewell
52 Bereft of boys
53 "We Will Rock You" group
54 Spokes, e.g.
58 Anti-Antony orator
59 Long Island town east of Bay Shore
60 New Hampshire town

61 Like colds
62 Emulates Rembrandt
63 Leathery-pod legumes
64 Truckers with handles
65 It's squiggly in São Tomé
66 Coral groups
67 Coccyges neighbors
71 One, after a decimal point
72 Fuel econ. rater
73 *People* mag subject
74 Palpate
75 Type of surgeon
76 Word maven Willard
78 Airhead
79 Approve formally
80 Fan sound
82 Certain reamers
86 Respond to an alarm
87 Baby blue, e.g.
88 Bushed, poetically
89 Bean Town ballpark
91 ER personnel
92 Ranchero's rope
93 Dig find
94 "There's nothing ___!"
95 It folds for lunch
96 Ratio phrase
97 In brogues
98 River of Switzerland
101 Bus. env. abbr.
102 Nerd
103 Hockey's Bobby et al.
105 Pre-school group?
107 P.I., e.g.
108 Suffix meaning "full of"
109 Botanist Gray

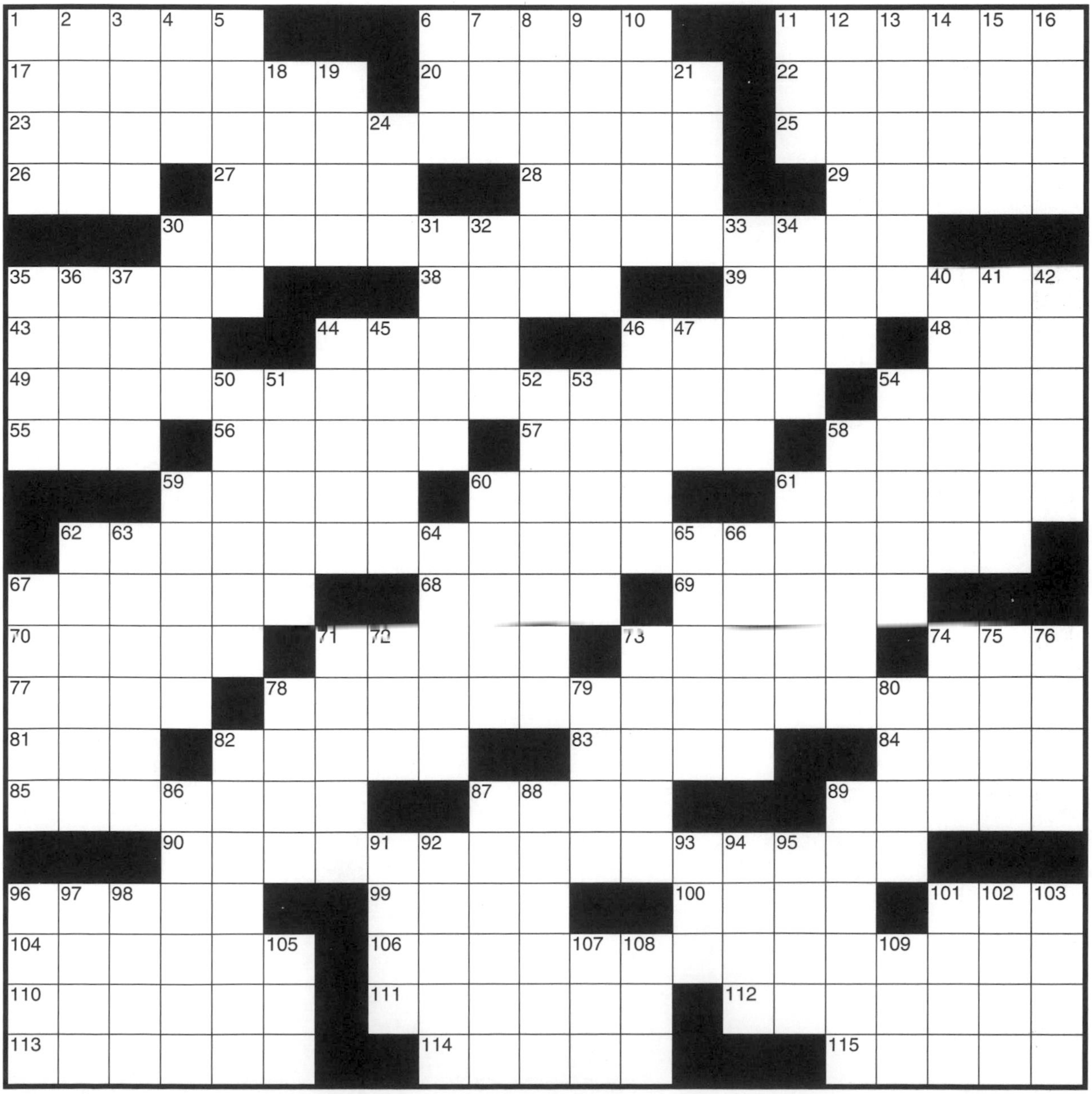

ANSWER, PAGE 83

WHAT A RIOT!
The visual kind

When this puzzle is solved, the shaded letters will spell out, in order, what the answers to the capitalized clues have in common.

ACROSS

1 With a bow, in the pit
5 Pointed end
9 *High Hopes* lyricist Sammy
13 Food for a baby, maybe
16 Bread
18 Mine, to Marcel
19 Stacking contest cookie
20 Letters for some messengers
21 *STAR WARS* "BATTLEFIELD"
23 With 58-Across, POPULAR KIDS' DISH
25 Sells directly to consumers
26 Stuff stuff (into)
28 Lawyers, collectively
29 Place whence French fly
30 Held note or rest
32 *B.J. and the Bear* sheriff
33 Weak and small
35 Sweet-pulped pod
36 Eye, to a poet
38 Ship-shaped clock of yore
39 Mandela's org.
40 Out of kilter
42 LARGEST WILD MEMBER OF THE CANINE FAMILY
45 Manuf. label abbr.
46 One's position, figuratively
48 Author Anita from India
49 DAYBREAK PHENOMENON
51 Adolph in newspaper history
54 Island near Corsica
57 Within, for a starter
58 See 23-Across
62 Russ.-built fighters
64 Spots for hops
66 Similar
67 DUGONG'S RELATIVE
69 Let up
72 Split, perhaps
74 It might move a mt.
75 SHOWINESS
80 Palindromic magazine
81 Tokugawa shogunate capital
82 Vegetable used like asparagus
83 Depend end
84 German philosopher Georg
86 Fiber source
87 Type of tetra
89 Like a fillet
91 Publicizes
93 Very nearly
95 Undo
96 Chivalrous phrase
99 PEA FAMILY VINE
101 BRISTLY SOMERSAULTER
103 *Wheel of Fortune* buy
104 Show a red flag
105 Plagues of Egypt component
106 1960s golf champ Sam
107 Longing
108 Hightailed it
109 Amuse to the max
110 Jazz's James or Jones

DOWN

1 Cupid
2 Lover-boy
3 FAIR TREAT
4 Name in Chicago Fire legend
5 Beanies, e.g.
6 Thurman of *Pulp Fiction*
7 Summer Olympics event
8 Old French mime character
9 Series mark
10 Latin altar
11 Metric land measures
12 *ER* actor Wyle
13 Gratis, as legal aid
14 Poe's "___ Lee"
15 Join or separate by twos
17 Seed coat
22 Artful
24 Theol. subj.
27 Both: Prefix
30 Clyde : Warren :: Bonnie : ___
31 Shakespearean choice
33 VCR remote button
34 Like many a hero
35 Tooth part
37 Bank of Scotland?
40 Communication at Gallaudet U.
41 Stop order
43 Gds.
44 Pebbles's mom
47 Bolt
50 *The Addams Family* father
52 X, to Xenophanes
53 Coop group
55 LIKE SOME ROMANCES
56 It may be converted to minutes
59 Arp's art movement
60 Minute
61 Countess's mate
63 First native-born American saint
65 Identical
68 Called-before-marriage
70 Links hazard
71 Leather finish
73 Listen to
75 Fugitive
76 Girl of barbershop quartet song
77 Focuses for a close-up
78 Enlai, Pinyin-style
79 Peaks
85 Of the knee
86 "Doctor My Eyes" singer Jackson
88 "Just kidding!"
90 Stigma
91 Half and half?
92 *Montreal* et al.
94 Puts in stitches
96 With skill
97 Ham is one
98 Work including the *Skalda*
100 Rage
102 Hamm of World Cup fame

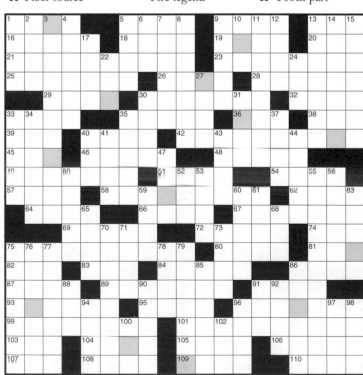

ANSWER, PAGE 85

GO FIGURE

When trying to solve this puzzle, do as the Romans do

ACROSS

1 Conk out
6 Tony
10 "Red-hot" ones
15 Way from one's heart
16 Dagwood's cousin
17 *A handful of snack items*
18 *Enough stones, say, for more than a thousand slingshots*
20 Home of Lafayette College in Pennsylvania
21 Subatomic particle
22 Actor Holbrook
23 Didn't let pass
24 Rachmaninoff or Prokofiev
26 Canadian hockey team
29 Company absorbed by Columbia Pictures
31 Buck's back?
35 Shelters
39 *What 100 stovetops would likely have*
42 Windward's opposite
43 When repeated, a Hawaiian fish
45 Month before Adar
46 *Early second-millennium tool*
49 *50 dozen jokers*
51 Temporary wheels, maybe

52 Feast with poi
54 *Winnie ___ Pu (classic book)*
55 *One-third of a case of wine*
57 Big cakemaker
60 Cape
61 As a group
63 Walking stick, for one
65 Contributing element
70 Powwow participants
73 Hawaii's ___ Day (May 1st)
75 *Rule, Britannia composer*
76 *Scoring perfectly in gymnastics*
77 *Groups of tests for the U.S. Senate*
80 Women-serpents of myth

81 Unseat
82 Dweller on the Bering Sea
83 Big jerk
84 Computer storage unit
85 Horseshoeing tools

DOWN

1 Groups on opposite sides of a dispute
2 Murderess Hart, Ginger Rogers role
3 Strong suit?
4 Smart
5 Takes in
6 Pet that gets potted
7 They often follow rings
8 Fury

9 With 77-Down, Connecticut town
10 *What a thousand kittens grow up to be*
11 Japanese detective's exclamation
12 Small amount
13 Two peas in ___
14 Taxpayer ID: Abbr.
17 Turn the wheel suddenly
19 Do some gathering
23 What "off" but not "on" may be
25 WWII arena: Abbr.
27 Hanker
28 Cry after "Well!"
30 Words with woe

31 Common problem during pregnancy
32 Charge over
33 Medium in antiquity
34 Germany's Nord-___ Kanal
35 Veep Hannibal
36 Room recess
37 Fixes up, for short
38 British bashes
40 Trojans' sch.
41 Spartan P
44 Dahl in films
47 Satisfied
48 WrestleMania wrestler
50 Give a damn?
53 Gomer Pyle's grp.
56 Minus
58 Comparable to a fiddle
59 Actor Stephen
62 Ultimately
63 *One ray of sunshine*
64 Sparks, Beatty, etc.
66 *Cheers waitress*
67 Attempts
68 Outdo
69 Stops on staffs
70 Pitfall
71 Avatar of Vishnu
72 "___ the east, and Juliet ..."
74 Diminutive suffix
76 Big T-shirt sizes
77 See 9-Down
78 Find believable
79 Corn serving

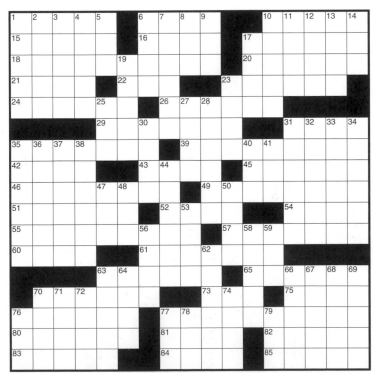

ANSWER, PAGE 87

NOT-SO-THIN AIR

A deletion gone awry

ACROSS

1 Amenable opposite
7 Deli assortment
12 Minnesota's Mall of America site
17 Camera : film :: eye : ___
18 More than fuzzy
20 Says "Wassup?," e.g.
21 Digital alternative
22 "Coats" made from "tacos," e.g.
23 They go for the gold
24 With 30-Across, Line 1 of a verse
27 Some H.S. students
28 Verb suffix
29 *Alfred* composer
30 See 24-Across
36 Designer Gernreich
38 *Mystery* host Diana
42 Sergeant who wanted "Just the facts, ma'am"
43 Score finale
44 Talbot of TV's *The Thin Man*
46 Hide-hare link
47 Let accumulate
48 With 64-Across, Line 2 of the verse
52 Result
53 Draw out
56 Son of Aphrodite
57 Trunk in one's trunk
58 Actress Harper of *Crimes of the Heart*
60 Janitor's finish
61 Intro Latin verb
63 Micro-organismic variety
64 See 48-Across
69 Summer sitcom, e.g.
72 Do "impressive" art?
73 Paris-to-Reims dir.
74 Goes down by the ocean
78 As regards
79 *Moonstruck* star
81 Assistants
83 Head of Great Britain?
84 With 105-Across, Line 3 of the verse
88 It may cause a wedding trip
90 Furor
91 Missing, but not "in action"
92 Peoples and Long
93 Minute
94 Fiddling emperor
96 Character in the comic strip "Nancy"
98 See 84-Across
100 With 105-Across, end of the verse
102 Even if, briefly
104 Org. concerned about PCBs
105 See 100-Across
115 Trevor or Bloom of films
116 Weird: Italian
117 Apparatus for getting black gold
118 Put down, slangily
119 All worked up
120 1960s folk-blues singer
121 Writers Lillian and Philip
122 Wheat species
123 Served ribs?

DOWN

1 Shrinking saltwater sea
2 Prefix with atrial or stasis
3 Info on touchdowns
4 Get a rise out of
5 Many a Currier and Ives
6 In a "Can't wait!" way
7 Name in Saigon's current name
8 Part of QED
9 Comparable to gold
10 Some start with rolls
11 Harder and dryer, maybe
12 Cuban lad in 2000 news
13 Kind of theater
14 Inkling
15 Egghead
16 Biblical beast
18 Crone
19 British record label
20 Professors ___
25 "This ___ stickup!"
26 The pits
30 Yesterday's plum
31 They make twists
32 Sch. in Norfolk, VA
33 Stalactite-like dripper
34 Perry Como hit of 1956
35 Domain name suffix
37 Nullify
39 Muscular prefix
40 Crime boss nicknamed "The Dapper Don"
41 Pun follower, perhaps
42 Guitar neck ridge
45 Onyx, for one
49 Blueberry's family
50 Art deco designer
51 Big band?
54 Eschew the fat
55 Labor grp. since 1935
59 Dictation taker
61 Elroy Jetson's dog
62 Abbr. near a jack
63 *Peter Pan* baddie
65 Form of yoga
66 "You can't do that, my user!"
67 River that joins the Oder
68 Common conjunction
69 Meir successor

70 Habituate
71 Thesaurus writer Roget
75 Mont ___ (highest of the Alps)
76 U.S. capital, literally "woody"
77 Matsushita competitor
79 Movement, for a start
80 Position of leadership
81 Stage actress Menken
82 Get out of the way
85 Spun
86 Civil War loyalty on the Blue side
87 Former Serbian capital
89 *The Crying Game* costar
93 It has underground branches
95 Wise-looking
97 Bring into harmony
99 Aberdeen river
101 *Monolith* and *Octopus* director John
103 President Grant's first name, originally
105 Medley
106 Donkey and elephant cartoonist
107 *Omni* subj.
108 It may have a fold
109 Belgian river
110 Submit
111 Supplication
112 Partner of sciences
113 Issue a summons
114 Mild oath
115 Naval rank below Capt.

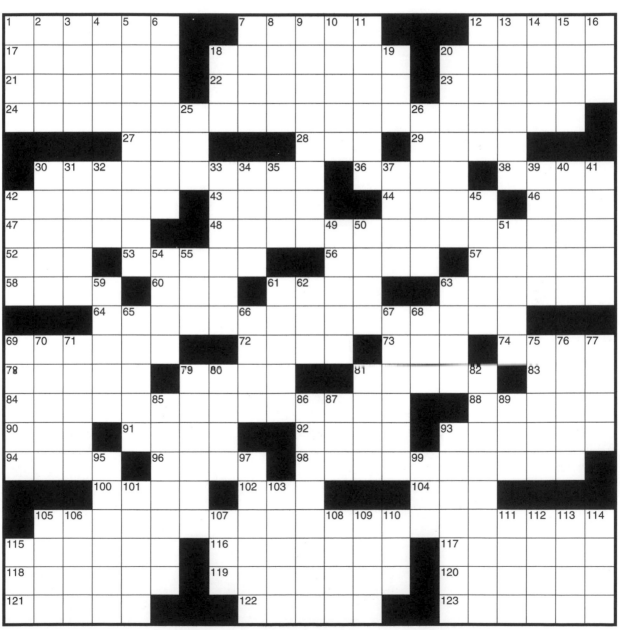

MILLHAUSER ANALOGIES TEST
And you thought the SATs were hard

ACROSS

1 Cathedral : clerical :: pew : ___
5 Castro : Batista :: Amin : ___
10 Henny Youngman : one-liners :: Roger Miller : ___
14 Hexa- : dodeca- :: tetra- : ___
15 Ticket : pass :: coin : ___
16 *Beethoven* : St. Bernard :: *Free Willy* : ___
17 225 : this puzzle :: 64 : ___
19 Diver : wet suit :: knight : ___
20 Polite : couth :: neat : ___
21 Seasoned : veteran :: green : ___
22 Em : Dorothy :: Bee : ___
23 Cretaceous : Mesozoic :: period : ___
25 Japan : kimono :: Malay : ___
27 Give forth : issue :: take back : ___
31 Unserrated : butter :: serrated : ___
34 Divine : forgive :: human : ___
35 White : black :: forbidden : ___
39 Maps : atlases :: anecdotes : ___
41 Bee : hive :: beaver : ___
42 Broccoli : cabbage :: cacao : ___
43 Arthur Wynne : crosswords :: Frank Lloyd Wright's son : ___

46 Safe : yegg :: joke : ___
47 Swiss cheese : holey :: cheesecloth : ___
48 Bell : jingles :: maraca : ___
50 France : châteaus :: Italy : ___
54 Branch : twig :: stream : ___
55 Letter : C :: man : ___
57 Plant : seed :: invention : ___
59 Manila : animal :: Seoul : ___
63 Duchess : duke :: countess : ___
64 Chips : French fries :: torch : ___
66 Gnus : news :: roos : ___
67 Disney World : Orlando :: Busch Gardens : ___
68 Ladder : rung :: louver : ___

69 Warsaw : Vistula :: Wroclaw : ___
70 *Norma Rae* : Sally :: *Carrie* : ___
71 Copperfield : magician :: Marceau : ___

DOWN

1 Jimmy : window :: pick : ___
2 Benadryl : itch :: Bengay : ___
3 Decide : dice :: emetic : ___
4 Magic : Puff :: Friendly : ___
5 Person who's not at a bank : ATM :: Person who's not at the racetrack : ___
6 Band : strike :: computer : ___
7 Shakes : nixes :: nods : ___
8 Greek : *geos* :: Latin : ___

9 ALF : Melmac :: Ewok : ___
10 Mozart : classic :: Brahms : ___
11 New York City : Yankee Stadium :: Miami : ___
12 ETA : arrival :: DNA : ___
13 Cagney : Gless :: Lacey : ___
18 Nametag : gateman :: parts : ___
24 Johnson : *Lives of the Poets* :: Thomas : *Lives of* ___
26 KGB : MGB :: CIA : ___
27 Circle : coterie :: sphere : ___
28 Oscar Madison : Felix Unger :: Bert : ___
29 Down : across :: descending : ___

30 Bottoms : *Tin Man* :: Boxleitner : ___
32 Saint James : Kate :: Curtin : ___
33 25-Across : Garson :: 31-Across : ___
36 John III : DLXI :: Julius III : ___
37 Addams : "Thing" :: Munster : ___
38 Nancy : Bushmiller :: Popeye : ___
40 "The West Wind" : Shelley :: "Joy" : ___
44 Dick Tracy : Trueheart :: Popeye : ___
45 Pound foolish : penny :: runs deep : ___
49 Mohammed : Islam :: Lao-Tzu : ___
51 Razes : flattens :: raises : ___
52 Lyndon : Barry :: Dwight : ___
53 Wood : joints :: cloth : ___
55 Ship : hydro- :: jet : ___
56 Ship speed : knot :: modem speed : ___
58 Scarabs : beetles :: Egyptian cobras : ___
60 Donkey and horse : mule :: grapefruit and tangerine : ___
61 Real McCoy : genuine article :: fake : ___
62 Juan : -ita :: Jean : ___
65 Bean : noodle :: sack : ___

78

ANSWER, PAGE 91

NO-BRAINER
This should be no problem

ACROSS

1 Main point
5 Extra
10 Indian cornmeal
14 Jon Arbuckle's dog
15 "Death Be Not Proud" poet
16 Having wings
17 What no good tennis player scores?
19 She was Sally in filmdom's *Cabaret*
20 Desserts that get lit
21 Gave consent
23 Manual reader
25 Texas's Sun Bowl site
26 Parental settings?
30 Superior
32 Its filling may be colorized
33 What no car affords?
38 Seasonal worker
40 Outboard motor inventor Evinrude
41 Toll
42 What no duck wants?
44 Colorado River feeder
45 ___ carotene (dietary hydrocarbon)
46 Tatooine or Naboo, e.g.
48 Like the Broadway show *Tru*
52 Antiquity
54 One brand is Royal
56 Mislead
61 They can drive ewe crazy
62 What no child of an actor Josh has in him?
64 Vermont, e.g., in Versailles
65 Behave effusively
66 Acronym re some couples
67 Business partners, perhaps
68 Eminent
69 Clearance sale admonition

DOWN

1 Volkswagen "sport-car"
2 Baal
3 Hindu god
4 Swarm
5 Like *Consumer Reports*
6 Use a divining rod
7 Threatening letters, to criminals?
8 "Watermark" singer from Ireland
9 Drop
10 Orchid tuber
11 Valli in *The Third Man*
12 They're hard to get out of
13 Home to Goya's *Naked Maja*
18 Come up against
22 Bob Cratchit is one
24 Road with ties
26 Shrinkage
27 Nation considered a rogue
28 It tells you what phone button to press
29 Mite
31 Word with sea or season
33 1940s kind of suit
34 Teri Garr's *Young Frankenstein* role
35 Sight for ore eyes?
36 *Vogue* rival
37 Part of a shutter
39 Slugger's turn
43 Inhabitant
46 Doc wannabe
47 Big name in building blocks
48 Shrek and such
49 "Peachy!"
50 Musician Mischa or Ziggy
51 Yard supports
53 Predecessor and successor of Amin
55 *Nautilus* builder
57 Roaster rater
58 Addiction to, in nonce words
59 Filmmaker Riefenstahl
60 Lodge brothers
63 Bosh

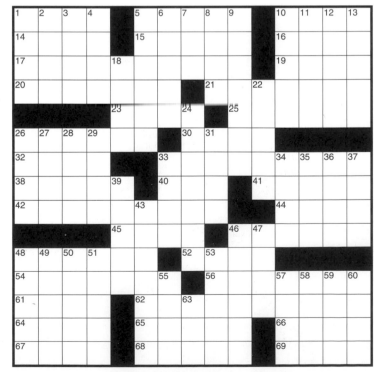

ANSWER, PAGE 93

79

LOVE THAT BLOB
Although he's a little hard to hug

ACROSS

1 *The Name of the Rose* setting
6 Bacchanalia
10 Common med. doses
14 Slangy "excellent"
17 Lindbergh kidnapper Hauptmann
18 Part
19 It may have a part
20 Second-largest cont.
21 The Blob's autobiography?
24 Dept. of Justice branch
25 Trivial amount
26 Telecommuter's office building
27 Pianist Gilels
28 They make history?
29 London-to-Ipswich dir.
30 Belt
31 Pour ___ thick
32 Dull, hollow thump
33 Damascene
35 Response to the Blob's fussiness?
38 Certain curtain feature
40 Diminutive suffix
41 Bares ears
42 Clyde Beatty was one
45 "Rushover.com" singer James
47 They're revolutionary
49 The Blob's theme song?
54 The folks
55 Gold: Prefix
56 Part of IRA
57 Socialite, British-style
59 What the Blob's enemies lobbied for?

65 Heloise with hints
66 Felipe's emphatic affirmative
67 TV's Maxwell Smart was one
68 Prickly plant
70 Rd. service provider
71 Valley of Ventura County
73 The Blob family's interactions?
77 Happen
81 City stray's hangout
82 "Your turn," to hams
83 1980 Nastassia Kinski title
85 Baseball's Berg or Drabowsky
86 Canasta move
87 Emoticon parenthesis, maybe
88 Department in northwest France

89 Chinese dynasty
90 Close rel.
91 What they said at the Blob's funeral?
94 Bud's comedy partner
95 Nitty-gritty
96 Shirt style
97 Pisan passion
98 Me Decade self-improvement program
99 Highland island
100 Relate
101 Ready to blow

DOWN

1 Bears
2 Eligible for Mensa
3 Bad-vibes happening
4 Suffix equivalent to -ity
5 Thou, now
6 Belted constellation
7 Had quarters
8 Crafts class blob
9 "Roundabout" rock group
10 Crime group nickname
11 Medical solution
12 Person who's hard to take
13 Box office letters
14 Strip of vestments
15 *The Newlywed Game* host Bob
16 Playful
22 Lake Geneva feeder
23 Volkswagen model
28 Actress Landi in 1930s films
30 Congo's name, for a time
31 Put down parquetry
32 Have value
34 Gossip tidbit
36 Equip with spars

37 Faith in Japan
39 Variety shows
42 Finger-pointer's sound
43 Dismounted
44 Van starter
46 ___ Haute, Indiana
47 White House "ruler" before Buddy
48 Designer Emilio and family
50 Filling station?
51 Nut
52 As to
53 Figurative high point
58 Short lunch?
60 Beefed
61 Impetuous
62 Delta rival, by its previous handle
63 Handles
64 Weekly interj.
68 Spanish dances
69 Flatten, as cookie dough
70 Responses from a flock
72 *The Pretenders* playwright
73 Speculate
74 Owner of the Lofoten Islands
75 Do the Wright thing
76 A walk on the mild side
78 River of booha?
79 Unsocial folks
80 Stowe novel villain
84 Matriculate
87 Oddball
88 Wide-ranged woodwind
89 It has a wide spine
91 Letters on U.K. hulls
92 Fitting
93 Bran source

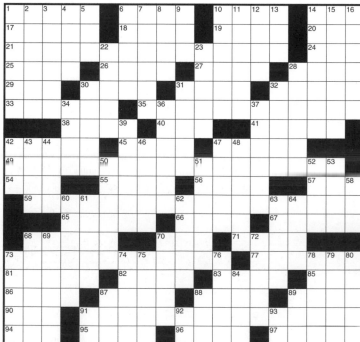

ANSWER, PAGE 95

43 CAMPING TRIP

```
O D D S . A R A B . . M A S T E R
T O R I . D E L E D . A L P A C A
T O A G R E A T E X . P O I R O T
O R T H O . T A B L E O F C O N S
. . . . S P A R . . L U T E . . .
. T O R S O . . S P I T . D A M E
L A A B I L I T I E S . C U M I N
A N T I . K A H N S . N A P A L M
N A B . P A L E A T H E R . T E E
A G R E E S . S T O O L . B E A S
T E A M S . P E R S I S C O U G H
E R N O . S O S A . . O H A R E .
. . . T A N G . . N I N E . . . .
M A L I C I O U S I N . A R U B A
O N E C U P . P I T C H T E N T S
R E V O T E . S T R U M . A D U E
T W I N E D . . S O S O . R O S A
```

52 COMBINING REFORMS

```
D A T U M . B E A R U P . J A M B
E L I S A . A R C A N E . A L I A
M E L D R A M A T I C S . W I L T
O X T A I L . . S A T E . E L M .
. . . . L E S . D I P S M A N I A
L I P O S U C T I O N . I D G E N
I R A Q . R A D . E D G E . . . .
N A N S E C O N D . M O R T I S E
E T D . C U B S . G E R E . L E D
S E A T T L E . B A R M E T E R S
. . . O O P S . O L A . R A T E .
G R O U P . T H E L O G I C A L .
R O T T I L L E R . D N A . . . .
A B S . C O I N . . . T U S S I S
Z E E S . S A D M A S O C H I S T
E R G O . E N E R G Y . H A L L E
S T O W . S A R T O N . O W L E T
```

62 INITIAL REACTION

```
Y O K E L . S C O O P S . M M D
A M I L E . O N A T O O T . O A R
W R E S T . L A P O F L U X U R Y
L I V E O N L I N E . I S I N . .
. . . . F O I L . C L A S S E . .
S C U F F L E . M E A L I N E S S
C O S E L L . R O L L I T . S A S
H I N D I . P O R T E N T S . . .
. L A U G H I N G O U T L O U D .
. . . P H E A S A N T . E L S A S
M R S . T E N O N S . C O V E N T
C O T I L L O N S . A L L E R G Y
H A R D Y S . . A R I D . . . . .
A N I L . . L A N D O L A K E S .
L O V E O R L E A V E . A F O R E
E K E . H E P A R I N . D R O N E
S E N . M A N D E L . Y O K E D .
```

71 TOPS

```
A I R S . B O L U S . S I G N I N
C R O C . E L E N A . A B R A D E
T W O H A N D E D P I N N A C L E
S I M O N . S K I I N G . P L E D
. N Y L O N . D E F R A Y . . . .
. . A D A I R . N O I R . R D A .
T U R R E T S A T T R A C T I O N
I N A . S A L S A . . S H A R K .
E S T E . L E A N T O S . E L S A
O U T R E . . G O R E N . T A R .
F R A N C I S F O R D C U P O L A
F E N . C M L I . T O T A L . . .
. . . R E P O R T . S N E E R . .
S O M E . A T E A S E . C A M E O
T H E B A C H M I N A R E T I N G
I N S U L T . A N I S E . E L A L
R O A S T S . N A T T Y . D E L E
```

6 UNSILENT PARTNERS

```
P I T . . J U N K . S P A S M
A C H E . A R O O . H E L L O
L A Y D O W N T H E O R D E R
E M M Y S . S E L L . F A W N
S E E T H E . . U S E . . . .
. . H A R D R O L L C A F E
H A L E . T O A D . O T T E R
E W E . L E N I E N T . T R I
L A S S O . O S L O . M A N E
M Y S Q U A R E L A D Y .
. . U S C . M O L E S T
G A Z E . I O N S . R O M E O
A B O A R D W I T H A V I E W
S I L K Y . E N Y A . E T T E
P E A S E . N E X T . S O L
```

16 VANISHING POINTS

```
A B E . R O L L . B E T E L
C O S . A R E A . S E L E N A
C H A I N I N G T H E C H
T R I N K E T . S P E N S E R
. E L L I O T . A A H
T I T L E . L U R I D . A M I
O R E L S E . T A P S . M E N
M O E S . R E D S . L P N S
E N T . C O R N . O T O O L E
I S H . L O N E R . A H O O T
. I D A . I D E A T E
F I N E S S E . C A T N A P S
A N E S S . P E R E A T E
D E G R E E . O D O R . R E X
E S S E S . L E N S . P R Y
```

25 UNMIXED VEGETABLES

```
S C A R . E L M S . S I D L E
H O R A . T O O T . K N E E D
O M E N . D Y N A M I C U D O
O M E G A . T I E D . S A M
K A L E S U P E R I O R
. D I N E . S N O O P E D
O B S . D I S K . M O R E
P L A N E T O F T H E P E A S
T O R E . C H E N . T S K
S C A R L E T . E X E S
. D E V I L Y A M C A R E
P S I . G E N O . Y E M E N
A N D Y E N D I V E . N O R D
S A L O N . E R I C . T R U E
S P E N D . R E N O . S E N D
```

34 IN BLACK AND WHITE

```
S A M B A . C H A R A D E . O A K U M
P L A I D . H O M E R U N . I V A N A
A P U Z Z L E L O V I N G C L E R I C
R O L E . A R T I E S . A E R A T E
. T I N Y . L E H R E R S
H O N . S A L A D . S U E S . E C H O
A T E S T . M O B . L E A N . R O W
W H O W O N H I M S E L F R E N O W N
K O N A . I O N I A N . R A C E S
. T E N D O N . T E R R O R
A M A H L . G O R D I E . N O R M
M A D E H I S R O B E S O F E I D E R
O R E . I N T O . S E E . L A D L E
S Y N C . T U T U . S L U M S . S Y D
. A T O N I N G . N O E L
C H O P I N . T R A U M A . O B O E
H E W O R E A C R O S S A N D D O W N
I R E N E . T R U S T E D . O G L E D
C O N E S . E Y E S O R E . M E A D E
```

44 GOING POSTAL

```
S L A M S   K I P S   D C O N
H A S A T   I D E A   R U I N
A S T R O   L O E B   I L L E
W H A T W I L L W E G E T
      E E L S   E R A S U R E
A L B S   L O D E   L U R E D
N A E   T O F U   A P A C E
A M A   I F F E D E X   L T S
L O R E N   T O N Y   L O S
O D I S T   C O O L   L Y R A
G E N T E E L   R A S E
      M E R G E S W I T H U P S
S H I V   G A E A   A R N I E
I O N E   E V R Y   F E D U P
L O D Z   D E B S   F R O S T
```

53 ALPINE SCHEMING

```
C O A S T   A S I A   E R O S
O S H E A   I N N S   N E V A
S L A L O M M A S S   U H U H
M O S A I C   F I E   M A L I
      S C H U S S K E B A B
M A E S T R O   T S A R
A B L E   E A T   N A T A L
T E L E M A R K G E T T E R S
S T A R E   T I P   E X I T
    S A C K   S H A S T A S
M O G U L L A T T E S
E X E C   A P R   B H O P A L
W I N K   S L O P E O P E R A
E D I E   S A V E   R E S I N
D E E R   A N E W   E C O L E
```

63 SKIP THE ER RERUNS

```
J U R A   E P P S   S O B E R
I R K S   A I R E   C R U D E
F L O W E R P O W   A D M I T
    A R L E N E   R O P E R
  D O N A   E R M A   E S O
A R Y   S C A T   A B B R
F O S T E R M O T H   A S A P
O N T A R I O   E L A N T R A
R E E D   K I L L E R D I L L
    R A T E   E A R P   C E E
O R C   A Y A H   E L K S
M O R A N   D R A G G Y
A B A C K   L E T T E R P A P
N I C H E   A R O O   I O W A
I N K E D   I S M S   C E L T
```

72 ANTHROPOMORPHIC ADDITIONS

```
F A S T S   A R T E L   U P S I D E
O R I O L E S   G U I N E A   L E H R E R
C O N T E N T D R E S S E S   M A R K E R
I N K   E D I E   S I C S   C U S P S
      O V E R W R O U G H T I R O N
T H E M E   E V E N   P I C K I E R
Y U R I   L E N I   C R A C K   M M I
R E S T R A I N E D S Q U A S H   R A P S
E Y E   O N C L E   O U S T S   C A R L E
    I O N I A   K N E E   V I D E O S
    E C S T A T I C E L E C T R I C I T Y
S T A L E S   B E E N   I E R E I
A C R I D   T E E N S   C L E A R   F O E
C H O P   D E P R E S S E D F L O W E R S
R E B   J O N A S   I L E S   H E A P
A S S A U L T   P A G E   F I L L Y
    W I T H D R A W N B U T T E R
I S A A C   O I S E   R O A N   A G O
S H A K E R   C A T A T O N I C W A T E R
T O R E R O   S T E R E S   T O A S T E R
O D E N S E   A L Y C E   Y A N K S
```

7 I SWALLOWED SOME BEES!

```
P E T E R   S L U R S     H E A L
A L A N A   Y A H O O S   A L T O
C H I C K E N H U M M U . . . O I S
T I L L E D   H U M M E L P I E
      A R O M A   L E A N   E R R
S L A V   M U R M U R   H A D E S
L A R E S   S E A S   C A N
O T T   P O S E R   T A N D E M S
T H E C A M E L S A R E C O M I N
H E L I C A L   A L O N E   D N A
      T E N   F L O W   S T E E R
M E D E A   M O A N E D   I N R E
A T E   G E A R   G L E E M
D O T H E L I M O     E X P O S E
C I A O   S L U M M E R P A R T Y
A L I T   E E L E R S   E N S U E
P E N S   D A N T E   L I O N S
```

17 YOU FIRST

```
A B I D E D   S I S     B L O C
V O L U M E   A L U M   R I T E S
E W I N G F A M I L Y   O C A L A
S L E D   S O A P S   W I R E D
      E U S T A C H I A N T U B E
  A L E P H         N N E
A D O   T O R S O   T R I B E
Y O O H O O I M H O M E   R U D E
A R K I N   M E A R A   R A N I N
H E A R   U S E R F R I E N D L Y
  S T E E N     E F L A T   L E A
      R I B       G A L E S
Y U K O N T E R R I T O R Y
A L O N E   N O O N E     C E N T
K N O T S   J U B I L A T E D E O
S A L A T   I T O S   C O U G A R
  E S P O   E T H   H O M E L Y
```

26 DIVISION OF LABOR

```
A L T A R   D E G A S   D E P O S A L
S E I N E   E X I L E   A D E L I N E
S A L E M   A U G E R   R I C A R D O
T H E W O R L D I S F U L L O F
      V A S E     P I E S   S A G
S A S H A Y   C A P O N   B E L L
E M A I L   W I L L I N G P E O P L E
A M A T   G E N I U S   S A L U T E S
R O B E R T F R O S T   T I T A N S
      A R T E     E T R E
T O D A T E   S O M E W I L L I N G
A Z A L E A S   E M I L I A   O D I N
T O W O R K T H E R E S T   Q U O T A
A N N E   E O S I N   O U T L E T
R E S   P E E P   J O N I
      W I L L I N G T O L E T T H E M
M I G R A T E   A L O U D   T H O L E
A L I E N O R   T U L L E   E E R I E
C A N N O N S   O G D E N   R O A S T
```

35 VEGETARIAN'S NIGHTMARE

```
T A M P   C R O N U S   J A B O T
E S A I   H O N C H O   A M A Z E
M E R C H A N T O F V E N I S O N
P A C K E R S     I C E   S N O
      S E R   O S I E R   M I E N
  V E A L O F F O R T U N E
H E F T     A T M S   E N D E D
A R F   S I R E E   R A V I O L I
I G O T P L E N T Y O M U T T O N
F E R R I E S   H A D E S   A P E
A S T I N   M I N E   S T E R
      B E E F E N C O U N T E R
T O M E   L E G G Y   P A R
A H A   O I D     E S T A T E S
B A R E F O O T I N T H E P O R K
B R I E F   R O C O C O   O R G Y
Y E A R S   A R I G H T   N O S E
```

84

45 DIG IT

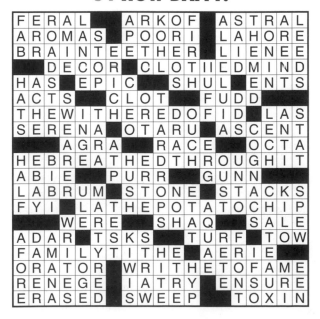

```
PETA .DIMS.PLAN
EVER.MOTET.RILE
RESTSONONESORES
UNTIES..ATTRACT
..SLED.CHIA..
.GETALODEOFTHIS
ORNE.LEE.LEANT
MED.SERVICE.NCO
NAOMI..IRE.SOAP
ITWASALLINVEIN.
..ETNA.STAN..
SKIWEAR.ANEMIC
MINERLEAGUEGAME
OWNS.ODDER.AXIS
GIST.GOAL.LINT
```

54 ONSET

```
HOWE ARCS ANKH EPSOM
OPAL SOAK IONIC LANDI
SEGA PACE DRAGONFLIES
TROMP DAIS SCHMO DOT
SAN ANTONCHEKHOV PENS
 THREE SHO ASIDE
 PROVOST MOAT ESSEN
SEASONTICKETS LECTURE
OKIE NOL BATONROUGE
SENDAK FRED ANDI MOD
 LEMONMERINGUE
SKA LEOI WINK PRISMS
CORDONBLEU LIT BTUS
OCTAVES STILTONCHEESE
THEME FEAR PILEATE
 PRIMA OAT NORMS
RUGS MARLONBRANDO OID
USE ARTOO EASY NANNY
MUTTONCHOPS UPIN CHAN
BAGEL HESSE MISO LANE
ALONE REIN ACHT UTES
```

64 HOW DAFFY!

```
FERAL ARKOF ASTRAL
AROMAS POORI LAHORE
BRAINTEETHER LIENEE
 DECOR CLOTHEDMIND
HAS EPIC SHUL ENTS
ACTS CLOT FUDD
THEWITHEREDOFID LAS
SERENA OTARU ASCENT
 AGRA RACE OCTA
HEBREATHEDTHROUGHIT
ABIE PURR GUNN
LABRUM STONE STACKS
FYI LATHEPOTATOCHIP
 WERE SHAQ SALE
ADAR TSKS TURF TOW
FAMILYTITHE AERIE
ORATOR WRITHETOFAME
RENEGE IATRY ENSURE
ERASED SWEEP TOXIN
```

74 WHAT A RIOT!

```
ARCO CUSP CAHN PAP
MOOLA AMOI OREO RNA
OUTERSPACE MACARONI
RETAILS CRAM THFRAR
 ORLY FERMATA LOBO
PUNY CAROB ORB NEF
ANC AWRY TIMBERWOLF
USA SHOES DESAI
SUNGLOW OCHS ELBA
ENDO ANDCHEESE MIGS
 GYMS AKIN MANATEE
 EASED SHARE TNT
RAZZMATAZZ ELLE EDO
UDO ENT HEGEL BRAN
NEON DEBONED AIRS
ALMOST RUIN ALLOWME
WISTERIA TUMBLEWEED
ANI WARN HAIL SNEAD
YEN SPED SLAY ETTA
```

The shaded squares spell CRAYOLA COLORS.

8 DOUBLE TAKES

```
L A B S   P R I M E D   C M D     P S S T
O B O E   D O R E M I   H I E R   U T A H
C A R R Y Q U I N T S   I N G E   R U D E
A I R E F I N I   H O N O R C R E D I T
L E O N A   S A U L   N A T A L E   Y E A
    W A R P   M O T E T     D E N I M
A S S     O P T   T I T O   E A T S U P
P H O T O G R A P H C O W S   N E L S O N
B E A R D   U V E A     N O B   E I R E
S A P I E N S   A R A B   L Y E S   C E O
      S U B S C R I B E T O A M A G
O T C   M A I A   O A H U   N O T E D L Y
D A H L   A R T     A B C D   A E R I E
E L O I S E   R E M O V E A B I N D I N G
  C O S T A R   L I L I   P Y M   N A G
    S T E R E   E N D O W     P E C K
U S E   A S T U T E   R A G S   L U C A S
S T A N D H I P H O P   R O C   U B O L T
H Y P O   O R S O   C O N T R O L A C A R
E L A N   T E E N   B R E T O N   N O R A
R I D E     D T S   S T R A D S   S A M P
```

18 BOARD GAME

```
E S A U   P D A       S M A R T
B E I N   A R N O     T A B O R
B E D S P R I N G   A R E N A
S P E L L   P A P E R C L I P
      A O L     U M B O
B A C K W A S H   M U S C A T
A L A E   I P E C A C   R I O
S A N D S   O R O   K I O S K
S R O   I N T E R N   C O L A
I M E L D A   S K A T E K E Y
    O E I L   P I P
B L A C K F O O T   D A N C E
R I C K I   S C O R E C A R D
A N T I C   S H O E   K N E E
S K I N K   O L D   S O W N
```

27 HORSING AROUND

```
R O T A   L O T T O     S T E P
O C H S   Q U O R U M S   T A P E
S H E S S U C H A N A G   A L P O
A R I A N A   P I N T O B E A N
S E R M O N O N   S I S A L
      T R E S       T E M P S
A D D L E   B A T T F R Y   I A M
S H E I L A   R I G A   R A R A
H A C K I N T O A C O M P U T E R
C R E E   K E E N   P E D A N T
A M I   C H A R G E R   Z E S T Y
N A T A L     E X A M
    N A D I R   T H E M O U N T
S T U D P O K E R   R O A M E R
P U R R   I N T H E S I C K B A Y
A B L E   T O R E O U T   E R R S
M E S A   W O O E D   N A S T
```

36 SAME DIFFERENCE

```
R E F I   L A T E   B A J A
O L I N   C I G A R   E X A M
W H A T S A F O U R   L I K E
S I T U A T E   A M U S E S
    I K E   C A N E S
L E T T E R W O R D W H O S E
U N O S   T A I L   L I N E R
N E T   C O R N E R S   E R A
C R E D O   T I N A   W A F T
H O M O P H O N E I S A L S O
    S T I N G   S I R
D A M A S K   P I L L A R S
I B E G   I T S A N T O N Y M
T I N E   N O U N S   C O N E
Z E U S   G E N E   K N E E
```

46 LAUGHTER EFFECTS

```
TRES   ESTAB  FOCI   BAUD
HELP  AREOLA  DART   ANNE
IFEELLAWFUL   AREALLOAF
SINEAD SUMMA  IDLE   MRI
 SACRE    NID NOONTIME
 HARDBOILLEGS   TRESS
IQS   MAIN   YIP   PIE
PUPS  EDGES  BEALLLEERS
SARTON  HOS  ELIAS  RUM
ADORN PRINTS ANT   TABU
 COOLLOTIONBREEZES
SIKH OID CLAIMS   EXUDE
EVE MONET  ARK  REARED
ISTHATYOUR  LITRE  SEMI
 ARS   BOG  NAIL   SOT
SPANS  DUALLAIRBAGS
LONGHAIR  EEL  BAUMS
ITO  ALPS XEBEC  ELNINO
CHILLLOUT  FINALLANCER
KENO  ALLY  UNZIPS  ERRS
SRTA  YEAR  LOONS   DODO
```

56 VERY-ATIONS

```
EGOS   CURB   POOCH
ARCH   OREO   RIFLE
RITEFANCY    ALFIE
STARRS  ODIN   AND
   PUTON  SCALES
SQUAMAE  STEN
EUR  PLUMWORNOUT
EASE  VEE   ATRA
PLANEORNERY   TAR
   VASE  PIANOLA
SATYRS   ASTRO
ADA  NAIL   ANTEUP
TASSE  REELSILLY
INTER  AUDI   OMAR
NOYES  ETON   NONO
```

65 SUSS OUT SEUSS

```
TAMPS  PRAM   OMAR
OPART  RULE   CUBA
FIGUREOFSNEETCH
UNISEX  FOOTLESS
   SWAG    ROO
GRINCHMEANTIME
SOYA  TEACH  SLAB
HUD   TSO    IDA
AGES  STOLA  BURN
YERTLEONEFORME
   RAE    SLOE
STRAITER   OLSENS
LAUNCHEDAWOCKET
OLEG  ELAN  NIEVE
WISE  SYST  GASES
```

75 GO FIGURE

```
CRASH  CHIC   MAMAS
AORTA  HERO   VCHIPS
MXMISSILES   EASTON
PION  HAL    VETOED
SERGEI  OILERS
  TRISTAR   AROO
HARBORS  CDBURNERS
ALEE  MAHI  SHEBAT
MCHAMMER  DCCOMICS
LOANER  LUAU  ILLE
IVBOTTLES  SARALEE
NESS   ENMASSE
  INSECT   FACTOR
  TRIBES  LEI  ARNE
XRATED  CBATTERIES
LAMIAS  OUST  ALEUT
SPASM   BYTE  RASPS
```

10 GYM DANDY

```
A B E T   P L A Z A   F E T A
L A S H   D A L E S   O X E N
V I C E S Q U A D S   B A N D
A L A R K   D E S I   E L S E
      L A I C     S U I T E S
T R A P S H O O T I N G
O A T Y   A N N E   U N P I N
O J O   S T E I N E M   A M I
K A R E N   A C T S   S L A P
      R I M L E S S S P E C S
S H E R P A       O I L S
C O X A   L O A D   T I T L E
O L I N   A B S O L U T I O N
W E L D   D I T T O   U N I T
L Y E S   Y E A S T   P E N S
```

19 IT HAPPENS WHEN ...

```
S T I N K S   K I G A L I   O R R S
E R M I N E   O C A R I N A   D U A L
P U P P E T S P U P P E T S   A N D Y
I I X   W I I D   D U H S   W I N
I S L E   M E S A   R E P R I C E
  M A N D R I L L S M A N D R I L L S
    O R D   U S A F   A N D E S
S T Y L I S T S S S T Y L I S T S
C H E A P   R A H S   O R E   O A H U
A O L   S C A L Y   T W E R P   J U S
M U L E   A P T   S E E N   O H A R E
  R A M P A R T S R A M P A R T S
E M A I L   N E U T   O I L
F A L C O N E T S F A L C O N E T S
F L A S H E R   F E E L   S I T S
E L S   A A R P   S O D A   M A A
C O K E   T A R G E T S T A R G E T S
T R A Y   S T O O L I E   W A L R U S
S Y N E   A P P O S E   G L O S S Y
```

28 TAKE IT WITH A GRAIN OF SALT

```
C L A M   S L A B   C I D E R
H E R A   P O L O   A D A G E
A M E N   L O G O   N Y L O N
F A N N I E M A N A C L E S
E N T I R E   E L A L
    K I N G S   I N O T E D
S T E I N   A K I N   I D O
P I N N A C L E N E E D L E S
U N D   A L I T   M I L N E
D E S E R T   N O N O S
    M E E K   E T H I C S
  G O B A R N A C L E F O O T
W E I L L   A V E S   U N D O
I N L E T   C O C O   L I A R
S T Y M Y   K W A N   S A S E
```

37 STRESS REDUCTION

```
L O I S   U C L A   P A A R
I T A L O   Z O O S   I N R E
S O M E T H I N G W I C K E D
P E S E T A   S A V A L A S
    P A R T   R I S E S
T H I S W A Y C O M E S
A I R   A S L A N   D O Z E N
G L O M   S E G A R   S I R E
S O N O F   R E G A L   N I X
    B L E S S E D E V E N T
A T S E A   R I T A
W R I T E R S   S T L U K E
H O M E S F O R T H E A G E D
A M O R   U R N S   R I L E D
M A R S   L E A K   S I P S
```

48 WHINE TASTING

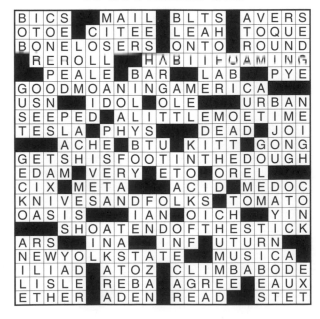

```
L E H R   S A R G E   R E C O N
O S E E   A L I A S   P E Y O T E
T A W D R Y P O R T   A L E R T S
S U N D A E   R E D B A R D O T
    F R S F   E E L Y   S I S
  S W E E T V E R M O O S E
P A A R   E L I S   C M O N
A M S   R E R A N   F A R A D S
S P A C K L I N G B U R G U N D Y
T A B O O S   F O S S E   T I N
A N I L   A O N E   F I S C
    L I E B F R A U M U L C H
A L E   S T I R   P U P U
B E A N O N O I R   R O B O T S
A N G E L A   C H E N I N B L A H
S T E E D S   A E R I E   E G G O
H O R D E   N A S A L   R A S P
```

57 THE TAMING OF THE DO

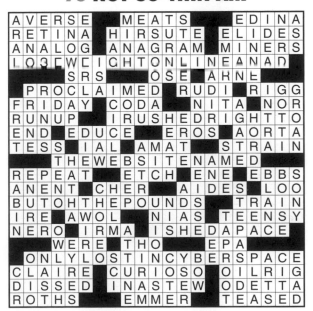

```
S T E A L   A S T E R   L E A
S H O A L E D   S P A R E   A D J
M O S T P E O P L E G E T   R I A
E T H O S   R E E D   L O G G E R
A G I N   S I R E   T O R A H
R U B   A N A P P O I N T M E N T
N A T H A N   B E G S   T E A
  H A R   D I E U   S T A Y
  A T A B E A U T Y P A R L O R
I N R I   D R Y S   L O U
C E E   E S A U   O D O R E D
I W A S C O M M I T T E D   P I G
  D E L O S   N A I R   C A M E
D I M W I T   U P T O   F A U N A
R O I   P H Y L L I S D I L L E R
O W L   S E E N A   E A R L E S S
P A L   E S S A Y   B E A T S
```

66 SOUTHERN-ORS

```
B I C S   M A I L   B L T S   A V E R S
O T O E   C I T E E   L E A H   T O Q U E
B O N E L O S E R S   O N T O   R O U N D
R E R O L L   H A B I T F O A M I N G
  P E A L E   B A R   L A B   P Y E
G O O D M O A N I N G A M E R I C A
U S N   I D O L   O L E   U R B A N
S E E P E D   A L I T T L E M O E T I M E
T E S L A   P H Y S   D E A D   J O I
  A C H E   B T U   K I T T   G O N G
G E T S H I S F O O T I N T H E D O U G H
E D A M   V E R Y   E T O   O R E L
C I X   M E T A   A C I D   M E D O C
K N I V E S A N D F O L K S   T O M A T O
O A S I S   I A N   O I C H   Y I N
  S H O A T E N D O F T H E S T I C K
A R S   I N A   I N F   U T U R N
N E W Y O L K S T A T E   M U S I C A
I L I A D   A T O Z   C L I M B A B O D E
L I S L E   R E B A   A G R E E   E A U X
E T H E R   A D E N   R E A D   S T E T
```

76 NOT-SO-THIN AIR

```
A V E R S E   M E A T S   E D I N A
R E T I N A   H I R S U T E   E L I D E S
A N A L O G   A N A G R A M   M I N E R S
L O S E W E I G H T O N L I N E A N A D
  S R S   O S E   A R N E
  P R O C L A I M E D   R U D I   R I G G
F R I D A Y   C O D A   N I T A   N O R
R U N U P   I R U S H E D R I G H T T O
E N D   E D U C E   E R O S   A O R T A
T E S S   I A L   A M A T   S T R A I N
  T H E W E B S I T E N A M E D
R E P E A T   E T C H   E N E   E B B S
A N E N T   C H E R   A I D E S   L O O
B U T O H T H E P O U N D S   T R A I N
I R E   A W O L   N I A S   T E E N S Y
N E R O   I R M A   I S H E D A P A C E
  W E R E   T H O   E P A
O N L Y L O S T I N C Y B E R S P A C E
C L A I R E   C U R I O S O   O I L R I G
D I S S E D   I N A S T E W   O D E T T A
R O T H S   E M M E R   T E A S E D
```

11 RUSH JOB

F	E	D	O	R	A	■	N	E	E	D	S	■	N	A	D	A
O	R	I	S	O	N	■	A	L	L	E	Y	■	O	V	A	L
X	M	A	S	M	E	R	C	H	A	N	D	I	S	I	N	G
Y	A	L	I	E	■	O	L	I	N	■	R	E	A	T	A	■
■	■	■	O	P	S	■	■	D	E	S	I	G	N	E	E	■
W	I	S	H	■	A	S	A	P	■	M	E	S	A	■	■	■
I	S	E	A	R	L	I	E	R	E	A	C	H	Y	E	A	R
L	A	D	I	E	S	■	R	E	L	I	T	■	■	N	B	A
L	I	A	R	S	■	M	O	T	E	L	■	A	T	T	A	R
O	A	K	■	X	E	B	E	C	■	A	T	R	I	C	E	■
W	H	A	T	L	L	N	E	X	T	A	W	A	I	T	U	S
■	R	A	I	L	■	T	S	A	R	■	M	Y	S	T	■	■
A	M	B	I	T	I	O	N	■	L	Y	E	■	■	■	■	■
B	E	A	S	T	■	E	A	S	T	■	M	A	N	G	O	■
E	A	S	T	E	R	E	G	G	N	O	G	C	H	E	E	R
A	R	I	A	■	O	T	E	R	I	■	R	E	A	M	E	D
M	A	N	N	■	D	A	V	I	T	■	R	E	B	O	Z	O

20 CUTESY

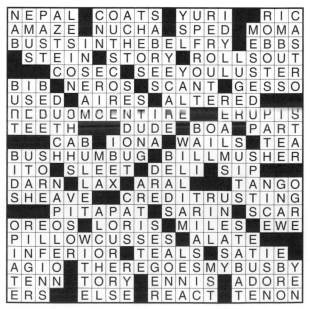

B	A	B	A	R	■	S	A	M	P	■	U	H	O	H
A	R	O	D	E	■	T	S	A	R	■	T	O	G	O
G	E	T	A	C	U	R	T	S	Y	R	E	P	L	Y
S	L	A	M	■	G	E	O	S	■	I	N	S	E	T
■	■	A	Y	L	A	■	A	R	T	S	■	■	■	■
T	E	E	N	S	Y	M	A	G	A	Z	I	N	E	■
A	L	A	T	E	■	M	E	G	■	L	I	S	P	■
P	E	T	■	R	E	H	I	R	E	D	■	G	T	E
S	N	U	B	■	R	A	G	■	O	S	H	E	A	■
■	A	P	A	T	S	Y	O	F	B	U	T	T	E	R
■	■	B	R	E	L	■	I	A	G	O	■	■	■	■
A	L	I	B	I	■	O	A	S	T	■	R	O	U	T
C	A	L	L	O	F	F	T	H	E	B	E	T	S	Y
E	D	I	E	■	A	T	M	E	■	O	U	T	E	R
D	E	A	R	■	T	S	O	S	■	S	P	O	R	E

29 ANIMAL TRAILS

O	P	E	C	■	G	E	S	T	E	■	B	R	O	S
N	O	R	A	■	R	E	P	O	T	■	O	O	P	S
S	L	I	P	P	E	R	Y	W	H	E	N	W	E	T
■	O	C	T	E	T	■	■	A	S	S	N	S	■	■
■	■	I	K	E	S	■	R	I	T	A	■	■	■	■
S	C	H	O	O	L	C	R	O	S	S	I	N	G	3
I	R	E	N	E	■	O	U	S	T	■	O	R	I	■
T	E	D	S	■	A	R	R	A	S	■	D	R	A	G
A	D	D	■	H	E	I	L	■	F	E	T	C	H	■
R	O	A	D	W	O	R	K	1	0	0	F	E	E	T
■	■	R	I	P	S	■	E	R	N	E	■	■	■	■
A	L	I	A	S	■	■	A	D	R	O	P	■	■	■
D	A	N	G	E	R	O	U	S	C	U	R	V	E	S
O	T	R	O	■	E	A	S	E	L	■	E	E	K	S
S	E	E	N	■	S	T	A	T	E	■	D	R	E	W

38 U S OF A

N	E	P	A	L	■	C	O	A	T	S	■	Y	U	R	I	■	R	I	C
A	M	A	Z	E	■	N	U	C	H	A	■	S	P	E	D	■	M	O	M	A
B	U	S	T	S	I	N	T	H	E	B	E	L	F	R	Y	■	E	B	B	S
■	S	T	E	I	N	■	S	T	O	R	Y	■	R	O	L	L	S	O	U	T
■	■	C	O	S	E	C	■	S	E	E	Y	O	U	L	U	S	T	E	R
B	I	B	■	N	E	R	O	S	■	S	C	A	N	T	■	G	E	S	S	O
U	S	E	D	■	A	I	R	E	S	■	A	L	T	E	R	E	D	■	■
R	E	D	U	O	M	C	E	N	T	I	R	E	■	E	R	U	P	T	S
T	E	E	T	H	■	■	D	U	D	E	■	B	O	A	■	P	A	R	T
■	C	A	B	■	I	O	N	A	■	W	A	I	L	S	■	T	E	A
B	U	S	H	H	U	M	B	U	G	■	B	I	L	L	M	U	S	H	E	R
I	T	O	■	S	L	E	E	T	■	D	E	L	I	■	S	I	P	■
D	A	R	N	■	L	A	X	■	A	R	A	L	■	T	A	N	G	O
S	H	E	A	V	E	■	C	R	E	D	I	T	R	U	S	T	I	N	G
■	P	I	T	A	P	A	T	■	S	A	R	I	N	■	S	C	A	R
O	R	E	O	S	■	L	O	R	I	S	■	M	I	L	E	S	■	E	W	E
P	I	L	L	O	W	C	U	S	S	E	S	■	A	L	A	T	E	■
I	N	F	E	R	I	O	R	■	T	E	A	L	S	■	S	A	T	I	E
A	G	I	O	■	T	H	E	R	E	G	O	E	S	M	Y	B	U	S	B	Y
T	E	N	N	■	T	O	R	Y	■	E	N	N	I	S	■	A	D	O	R	E
E	R	S	■	E	L	S	E	■	R	E	A	C	T	■	T	E	N	O	N

49 THINK OUTSIDE THE BOX

58 ABSOLUTELY BUSHED

68 SPACE CRAFT

78 MILLHAUSER ANALOGIES TEST

12 TRIPLE FEATURE

```
B L A B S   C A L F   A R A B
A S S E T   U V E A   R I L E
G U A V A   B O N D   I C O N
        E Y E S W I D E S H U T
    E R R O L   S N I D E
C L E A V E S     S U N N E D
H A N G E M H I G H     A L A
E I D E R   O L A   A S T I N
A N E     D E E P I M P A C T
T E R E S A     S T E E L I E
      D E W A R   I N L E T
    3 D I M E N S I O N A L
W A C O   S I V A   B O A R D
A D E N   O D E R   L U C C I
Y A R D   N E T S   E T H A N
```

21 OVER THERE

```
P A R K A Y   D A I S   A B B R
A S H O R E   E N N U I   A R I A
R H O N D A   M I C R O C H I P S
D E N     R O O S     T A S T E E
O N E M I N U T E F L A T   I D S
    E L S I E   E A S E L S
I M P E L   S P R Y   R E H A B
N E U R O N S   A M O I   D I N E
A L S   F A C E L I F T S   S T A
N O S H   E R L E   F O O T M A N
E N I A C   E I R E   E A S E S
    N I E C E S   R A O U L
O T B   L U N A T I C F R I N G E
R O O T E R   E T T A   O H S
S N O W B L O W E R   R H O D E S
O N T O   S H O N E   T U L A N E
N E S S   M E S A   S M E L T S
```

30 OLDIES

```
H A R M S   N E A P   A D D O N   E C O L
A X I A L   E B R O   L A R G E   X L V I
W E D D I N G B I L L B L U E S   P A I N
S L E E P E R   D E E   I G E T R O U N D
      O T I S   C A A   S A S S E S
G R I E F   I N A S N I T   C U E S
L E T S F O R G E T T O G E T H E R
I M A C   N I N E   D O N E E   E Z R A
B O L A   C O L D O   T E A M   S E A N
    P O E T R Y I N M O T R I N   A I D
A D I E U   K I A   N E L L Y
D I N   I F O U G H T T H E L A W N
A N T I   A R N O   S A L E M   J O W L
M O O N   L A I R D   T R I O   O M O O
    I C A N T S E E C L E A R L Y N O W
S E T A   S E A L I O N   A S I D E
A T T I L A   L I T   O M I T
N O H A I R M A N   O R E   E M E R I T I
D R A T   D A N C E T O T H E P R O Z A C
R E N E   O T T O S   N A B S   A M O C O
E Y E S   R E E S E   S L O E   L E D O N
```

40 APT APPELLATIONS

```
P O C K E T   B L A Z E   C A P O
I R O N E R   R I S E N   O R A N
T A R A L I G A M E N T   O A T Y
S L A V   U V E A   H A T B O X
    T E C H I E   B U L   L I E
C R O   H E D D A B U S I N E S S
R U M M A G E   S L E E V E
E L A I N E   S O N   E A M E S
S E T S   L I S A C A R   R O L O
C R O A T   L O U   O P E N E R
    C O S E L L   A V E R A G E
C H I T A C U S T O M E R   L Y S
L A C   D A M   R O S T R A
E V E L Y N   S I G N   A M O S
R A C E   D O N N A G A R M E N T
G N A T   A D O R N   B O U N C E
Y A P S   L E W I S   S Y S T E M
```

50 PERSONAL COMPUTING

D	O	A		W	R	A	P		H	E	L	M		M	A	D	A	M
E	A	R	P	I	E	C	E		O	D	A	Y		S	U	A	V	E
P	H	I	A	L	N	O	T	F	O	U	N	D		U	T	T	A	R
P	U	L	E	D		W	T	O		C	O	B		O	E	I	L	
		A	L	P		Y	O	U	V	E	G	O	T	M	A	L	E
C	R	A	N	I	U	M		F	R	I	T		G	R	A	R	
A	O	L		F	R	O	M	A	G	E		A	G	I	T	A	T	O
M	O	T	H	E	R	B	O	R	E	D		B	L	U	E	S	K	Y
S	M	E	E		I	R	A	S		A	D	E	N		S	O	S
	R	E	P	L	O	W		C	R	I	S	E	S	
O	K	S		E	R	I	N		L	A	I	C		H	O	O	P
R	E	H	I	R	E	S		C	E	R	E	A	L	P	O	R	T	S
C	Y	A	N	I	D	E		H	O	L	S	T	E	R		N	I	A
	R	H	E	A		V	I	N	I		E	V	E	R	E	S	T
C	L	E	A	R	T	H	E	C	A	S	H		I	T	A	
H	O	W	L		E	E	N		L	E	E		E	N	O	L	A
A	R	E	A	S		C	U	R	S	E	R	C	O	N	T	R	O	L
I	N	A	N	E		H	E	E	L		D	R	E	S	S	A	G	E
M	A	R	T	A		E	S	P	Y		S	U	R	E		L	E	S

59 KNOCK IT OFF!

S	C	A	M		M	O	T	T		J	E	A	N			P	I	S
T	A	R	A		A	R	I	A		E	X	P	O		F	A	C	E
O	N	E	S	B	L	O	C	K		T	E	R	M	P	A	P	E	R
M	O	N	T	E	L		T	E	N	E	T		A	Q	A	B	A
P	E	A	S	E		R	A	T	A		E	S	P	Y		Y	A	P
				P	R	I	C	E	P	E	R	C	E	N	T	A	G	E
S	P	O	T		E	I	S	N	E	R		O	L	E	O	
C	A	R	A	C	A	S			N	A	T	E		N	A	D	A
A	R	C	T	I	C		A	T	B	E	S	T		O	G	L	E	D
R	A	H		T	H	E	D	A	Y	S	W	O	R	K		U	R	E
E	D	I	L	E		R	E	M	O	T	E		A	R	O	M	A	S
R	E	D	O		R	A	S	P				I	N	A	S	N	I	T
		D	A	I	S		E	B	B	I	N	G		S	A	L	E
D	E	S	I	G	N	E	R	D	R	E	S	S	E	S	
I	L	O		O	G	R	E		A	L	O	T		P	A	T	I	O
S	O	L	A	R		D	W	E	L	T		C	A	B	A	N	A
T	H	E	B	A	D	G	U	Y		Y	O	U	R	S	O	C	K	S
A	I	M	S		O	R	C	S		U	P	T	O		V	I	L	E
L	M	N		Z	E	E	S		P	E	E	P		E	T	E	S

69 HONEYBUNCH

J	A	G			F	O	S	S	A		R	A	S	P
A	S	I	F		O	P	A	H	S		E	L	L	A
W	E	L	L		R	E	M	O	P		T	A	O	S
S	A	L	U	T	E			T	R	A	U	M	A	S
			B	A	G	P	I	P	E	D	R	O	N	E
T	H	E	S	N	O	W	Q	U	E	E	N	
A	I	L		E	A	S	T		L	E	E	R	Y
F	L	A	M	E	S			P	E	E	W	E	E
T	O	N	I	C		S	T	L	O		O	N	A
		S	O	C	I	A	L	W	O	R	K	E	R
S	P	E	L	L	I	N	G	B	E	E	S	
C	L	U	E	I	N	G		R	O	V	E	R	S
R	A	R	A		E	L	V	I	S		P	H	A	T
I	Z	O	D		M	E	A	R	A		S	U	N	Y
M	A	S	S		A	T	L	A	W			D	I	X

79 NO-BRAINER

G	I	S	T		A	D	D	E	D		S	A	M	P
O	D	I	E		D	O	N	N	E		A	L	A	R
L	O	V	E	A	L	W	A	Y	S		L	I	Z	A
F	L	A	M	B	E	S		A	C	C	E	D	E	D
			U	S	E	R		E	L	P	A	S	O
L	I	M	I	T	S		A	O	N	E	
O	R	E	O		Z	I	P	D	R	I	V	E	S
S	A	N	T	A		O	L	E		K	N	E	L	L
S	Q	U	A	T	D	O	W	N		G	I	L	A
		B	E	T	A		P	L	A	N	E	T
O	N	E	M	A	N		Y	O	R	E	
G	E	L	A	T	I	N		B	E	G	U	I	L	E
R	A	M	S		Z	E	R	O	M	O	S	T	E	L
E	T	A	T		E	M	O	T	E		D	I	N	K
S	O	N	S		N	O	T	E	D		A	S	I	S

13 SMALL CHANGE

```
S H I V E R _ M C S _ A D A R
I O D I N E _ G A L A _ S E L E S
T H E _ _ C O R R A L _ C W I D E
S O A K _ M A I N E _ _ I C E D
_ _ I T H A D A G P R A T I N G
E S L _ O A R S _ _ E S T A T E
S L O U G H _ C R E D O _ _
P U T S O N A P A I R O F J P S
O R T S _ M A R N I _ O A H U
_ P O R T A B L E D C P L A Y E R
_ _ I V I E D _ L A D E R S
A R C A N E _ A T O I _ R E A
F I R S T C E N T U R Y C B _
O N U S _ R E A T A _ A B E T
O S I E R _ A V H O S P I T A L S
T E S S A _ T I O S _ U L T I M A
_ R E S T _ O L E _ T A Y L O R
```

22 NONVERBAL

```
D A T U M _ I T C H _ C H I L I _ A L D O
A L I B I _ N O R A _ L A G E R _ T E E D
O R D I N G S E V P U L N N E R _ H A U L
H O E _ C U T U P _ E N D O R _ P A V E S
_ _ C E R E _ M I T E R _ A L T E R S
R O L L S U P O N E S S L E E V E _ S T A
E R I E _ N E A T _ _ R E A T A _
C R E E P S D O W N S T A I R S _ E T T E
_ S L Y E S T _ R U S S _ D E F E R
_ S H E E N A _ F R I T O _ S O N O M A
I T O _ B O L T S O U T O F B E D _ U P S
B O P P E D _ A C U T E _ E D G A R S
M O S E S _ O R A N _ I M A G E S
S P I N _ S T A N D S O N O N E S H E A D
_ N A O M I _ H O R A _ _ I M R E
E F T _ D U C K S B E H I N D T H E B A R
G E H R I G _ I C E R S _ A U E R
G R E E N _ A D L A I _ W O R S T _ T A U
M U T E _ H I D E S F R O M T H E C O P S
E L U L _ I N E R T _ D U N E _ R O U S E
N E B S _ J U D A S _ S K I D _ O T T E R
```

32 WHERE THEY STAY

```
J E S T _ A M O S _ P R O W L
U T A H _ N O A H _ I O N I A
T A K I N G T H I N G S I N N
S T E R E O _ U N O P E N E D
_ _ D E L I _ E V E _ _
A I M _ S A N G _ E N I G M A
D R A N O _ B O I L _ D O E S
L A Y I N G O F F S U I T E S
E T O N _ O X E N _ N O O S E
R E S O R T _ R O M E _ N E T
_ _ A H S _ T E S T _ _
I R R I G A T E _ S C O U R S
B E I N G M O R E H O S T E L
I M A G E _ R I L E _ C E D E
D O L E D _ K E Y S _ A P O D
```

41 CASEWORK

```
M A F I A _ C A I N _ J A I L
E L A N D _ Z U N I _ E N Z O
W O R K O F A T V L A W Y E R
L E M _ N E R O _ _ B E A R D
_ _ _ E A R _ P A I L _ _
P L A Y I N G C A R D S B O X
R I D E S _ L O R N E _ A M E
O V I D _ R I N S E _ B L A B
N E E _ S A D I E _ A L E N E
G R U M P Y E C C E N T R I C
_ _ _ A U E R _ W D S _ _
A C O R N _ A G E R _ I D O
Q U I C K L Y C U R E D B U G
U R S A _ B E E S _ W E I L L
A B E L _ S A S H _ S I D L E
```

51 THE WORKS!

```
MARS   APIAN    EDIT
ALOU   FIONA    YENS
SOUPTONUTS      ELLA
STEPOUT    SHATTER
    LILAC      MEATS
LAPEL     AEGIS
EMU   STEMTOSTERN
ABRA   ALINE    SHOE
FIRSTTOLAST     UPI
    TRAIL    AUDEN
KAZOO     EVENS
AGENDAS    INGESTA
SARI   HEADTOFOOT
ENOS   ALTER    UNDO
MASH   SAVOY    LODZ
```

60 MR. HOLLAND'S OPUS

```
JAMB   TRON   ESAS    TWERP
IDEA   HULA   PLUMS   MODEL
FORTHEHAGUEOFIT       ALIVE
   HEIR   ANEW   LOAN   TED
DOWELS   IND   GAELS   SONG
UGH   ITSTOOGOUDABETRUE
TEAROSES   LIT   AROSE
YETI   GARDENOFEDAM
   AGORA   HANGSON   SAMOS
ALBINO   WETS   RTE   ITO
WOODENSHOE   LIKETOKNOW
OLE   SEA   SOLS   TORTES
LARCH   GRISTLE   DEPOT
   OUTOFGUILDER   NUIT
   BURGH   LPN   TESSELLA
VERMEERTOETERNITY   ISR
EGGS   FUROR   MAA   INAPET
SUE   ATTU   GLUT   FROG
TIDAL   HESLOSTHISDUTCH
ELOPE   STOUT   AUDI   SOHO
DENTS   ODES   NEON   HEED
```

70 PLAY WITH YOUR FOOD!

```
LIZA   BUDS   AMMO    STU
AMID   ERAT   SAAB    WHOS
MANDOLINORANGE        OATS
ACCENT   ULA   DISORDER
   RASPBERRYCELLO
ARI   RENEE   EDWIN
PINHOLE   ABACI   BSE
OCTAVES   DILLPICCOLO
DOODAD   SOL   APT   OXEN
   FLUTECOCKTAIL
ESAU   PET   NYE   DRAWLS
SPINETSALAD   HEADIER
ACR   LOTTE   ALSATIA
SAMOA   NATCH   HAS
   ARTICHOKEHARPS
MAIDENLY   INA   EYELET
UGLI   TEAANDTRUMPETS
TREE   RATS   ETAS   TATA
TAD   ANTS   DYNE   ADAR
```

80 LOVE THAT BLOB

```
ABBEY   ORGY   TSPS   DEF
BRUNO   ROLE   HAIR   EUR
IAMCURIOUSJELLO        FBI
DIME   HUME   EMIL   ERAS
ENE   ZONE   ITON   CLONK
SYRIAN   DONTBESOICKY
   TIER   ULA   HUSKS
TAMER   ETTA   SPINS
SLIMEEVERYMOUNTAIN
KIN   AURI   ACCT   NOB
   TIGHTERGUNKCONTROL
   REESE   SISI   AGENT
BRIAR   AAA   SIMI
GOOPDYNAMICS   BEFALL
ALLEY   OVER   TESS   MOE
MELD   GRIN   ORNE   TANG
BRO   HEWASABORNOOZER
LOU   MEAT   POLO   AMORE
EST   SKYE   TELL   TENSE
```

14 BRIDGE CROSSINGS

```
SCOFFS OLIN LARD AMES
KOREAN MIRO OMAR TAFT
ICANTILEVERALONE AUNA
MULE PAGE PIU SALVER
  SHECANOUTTRESTLEME
SORTERS STP ASSET
KNURL URAL TRIPPER
IBEAMCOMPATIBLE CARVE
SYD SLOE NAISH SEED
 MONA ARECA USHERS
 HEHASANTSINHISSPANS
DEVINE DISCS SITE
AMID SEENA OKLA PRO
DICER CRYINGINHERPIER
ONTRIAL LAIN MOTEL
 SNAPS NBC ALERTLY
THEKEYTOMYABUTMENT
RODENT DIA ROOT ERGO
EVIL IPUTMYTRUSSINHIM
NELL MANE EWER UNDONE
TREY ELKS WADS PASSON
```

24 GIMME A LIFT

```
COMP STEAM ABLE
OBOE HALLE GAOL
HOUSIERBED ENDS
ATSEA TAXI LAZE
NETTLE CAEN
  ACRANEOFSALT
HESS ALES ASNER
AST STOUTER UVA
RAISE OREL QTIP
PULLEYFORYOU
 LAKE SPINES
JOLT NENE ENOLA
EDIT TWOWINCHES
FIFE AARON EINS
FEED SNAKE STAY
```

33 IN THE BALANCE

```
LOAF AIDES RAMP
EMMA DAVIT ITAL
TOUCHANDGO NEMO
TOREUP HANGSBY
 INTACT ALTOS
HAST MOHAVE
EXE LION LITTLE
REMAINSTOBESEEN
ALINES ALAS RAD
 ANOMIE PINS
OSAGE UNSAFE
ATHREAD GOOGOO
ROMA UPFORGRABS
ELAM NIOBE IRIS
DADS TEPEE AREA
```

42 THE SCOOP

```
SPCA TRASH ESPANA
IRON SHERPAS REUSES
ZOOT PEPPERMINTTICK
ENTO RAE WEAN STAKE
SAINT SAD LANA NSW
UTE MAPLEAWLNUT
PECTEN ANIOEN EWOK
NUNO ATEN CHERRY
ARCO MOCHAGYP ONEAL
DOR EARL OLAY NNE
OLEIC BUBBAGUM ACTS
PLAQUE RUDI AMAH
TOMS DESIRE NERVES
 PUTTERPECAN ANY
MBA ACHY TAR DENTS
ARGOT ELIO RUE DIRT
HEATHBRACRUNCH GLEE
RATIOS RENTEES ELAM
EDESSA SEARS RATS
```